Resources for Teaching
Contemporary & Classic
ARGUMENTS

A PORTABLE ANTHOLOGY

Sylvan Barnet • Hugo Bedau

Resources for Teaching

CONTEMPORARY & CLASSIC ARGUMENTS

A Portable Anthology

Resources for Teaching

CONTEMPORARY
&
CLASSIC ARGUMENTS
A Portable Anthology

SYLVAN BARNET

HUGO BEDAU

Bedford/St. Martin's   Boston ◆ New York

Manufactured in the United States of America.

9   8   7   6   5
f   e   d   c   b   a

For information, write: Bedford/St.Martin's, 75 Arlington Street, Boston, MA 02116   (617-399-4000)

ISBN: 0-312-43629-7

EAN: 978-0-312-43629-2

Preface

Like the book they accompany, these notes are the work of two people — one a teacher of literature and composition, the other a teacher of philosophy. No single set of notes can fully satisfy all instructors or even be of much use to all instructors, but we hope that our alliance has enabled us to produce some notes that will have something of interest for almost everyone.

The Scope of These Notes

If the two of us have succeeded in being of some use, it is partly because we have different approaches and partly because we do not methodically treat every anthologized essay in the same way. We treat *all* of the essays — some briefly, some extensively, some chiefly from a rhetorician's point of view, some chiefly from a philosopher's point of view. We have, however, always kept in mind that because teachers of composition courses devote many hours to reading students' papers, they have correspondingly fewer hours to devote to working up the background for unfamiliar essays. We have therefore provided background on such matters as affirmative action, the death penalty, gay marriage, and sexual harassment, so that an instructor who happens to be relatively unfamiliar with one or another of these topics nevertheless can teach with ease the essays we reprint.

Beyond providing background on specialized topics, in these notes we simply touch on some of the matters we discuss in our classes. We realize that something is artificial here; what one does in class depends heavily on the students and on the stage in the term at which one is studying an essay. And of course what one does in class depends even more heavily on one's ideas of what teaching is. Still, we hope instructors will scan these comments and will find at least some of them useful; if the comments seem utterly wrongheaded, they may nevertheless be useful in providing material to react against.

EXERCISES

All of the essays and literary selections in the text are followed by exercises, but in these notes we include some additional topics for discussion and writing.

Contents

Part Two

CASEBOOKS ON CONTEMPORARY ISSUES

Resources for Teaching

CONTEMPORARY
&
CLASSIC ARGUMENTS
A Portable Anthology

Part One

DEBATES ON CONTEMPORARY ISSUES

1
Affirmative Action: Is It Fair? (p. 3)

From its inception nearly forty years ago in President Johnson's Executive Order 11246 (1965) to the present moment, affirmative action has been one of the most controversial set of social programs created by federal law and practiced, voluntarily or not, in countless industries, businesses, and offices. These programs were a natural outcome of the civil rights movement of the 1960s, once it was realized that purely formal equality of opportunity (that is, nullification of legal segregation and Jim Crow laws) was not by itself enough to ensure progress of minorities in all avenues of employment and careers. Something else was needed, and needed promptly, if the promise of "equal opportunity" was not to be a mockery for those so long denied any opportunity because of their race and color. Affirmative action programs — with their "minority set-asides," "goals," and "quotas" — were the result.

Affirmative action as it affects (white) women was a parallel development and to date has been far more successful by every measure in advancing the interests of women than have been those programs designed solely to increase equality of opportunity for nonwhites.

Affirmative action continues to be in the forefront of domestic political controversy. One of the most prominent arenas of controversy is college admissions. In California, Proposition 209 (prohibiting race as a factor in determining public college admissions) has resulted in a severe drop in the enrollment of minority applicants (excluding Asian Americans, who do extremely well in competition with every other group of applicants, including whites). *Time* reports (April 20, 1998) that African Americans, Native Americans, and Latinos, who together constitute 34 percent of the state's population, amount to only 10 percent of that year's admissions. According to a report in the *New York Times* (April 12, 1998), however, this has stiffened the spine of advocates of affirmative action. The *Times* also reports (April 5, 1998) that anti-affirmative action legislation like Proposition 209 was defeated in thirteen state legislatures during 1997. And (according to the same source) it has caused prominent neoconservatives, such as James Q. Wilson and Nathan Glazer, to rethink their hostility to affirmative

1

action. Only yesterday they shared the outlook of Terry Eastland (see the text at p. 3); now they are reported as having suddenly realized that affirmative action in college admissions is the only way to prevent thousands of African American youngsters from losing their best opportunity to enter the middle class.

Those users of our text who would like to see a fuller account of the actual effects of affirmative action as measured by the available statistics should consult the tome by Stephan and Abigail Thernstrom, *America in Black and White* (1997). Their reading of the data convinces them that considerable progress in raising the accomplishments of African Americans over the past generation owes little or nothing to affirmative action. Not surprisingly, several reviewers of their book have severely criticized that interpretation.

Terry Eastland

Ending Affirmative Action (p. 3)

When Terry Eastland says (para. 6) that "we do not have to take the risk of affirmative action," we wonder what alternative he proposes that is less risky (see our question 3). (Could it be that he just wants minorities to work harder and score higher — and if they fail, then what?) Just what measures within reason could we adopt, after abandoning all forms of affirmative action, to improve prospects for equality of opportunity for African American youths?

Here's a thought, not original with us but worthy of class discussion: Why not adopt new policies of college admission, for example, where the basis for special admission advantages is not race but socioeconomic class? What would the details of such a program look like? (For example, we could give an edge on admissions to applicants whose parents earn less than $30,000 and who are not themselves college graduates.) Would Eastland attack that kind of alternative, too? (After all, poor people are disproportionately black, and conversely.)

Eastland, like other critics of affirmative action, is quick to blame such programs for "encourag[ing] Americans to think of themselves in racial and ethnic terms" (para. 11; cf. our question 7). Does he mean to imply, or suggest, that until such programs were invented in the 1960s, Americans never (well, hardly ever) thought of themselves in racial terms? Perhaps today's college students, who have never known our society without affirmative action programs, might be inclined to agree. But others like us, who grew up in racially segregated America, knew from earliest youth what it was like to "think in racial and ethnic terms." It would be an outrageous distortion of the facts to put the blame for that error (if error it is) on three decades of affirmative action.

Burke Marshall and Nicholas deB. Katzenbach

Not Color Blind: Just Blind (p. 11)

During the 1990s, affirmative action was subject to widespread criticism and some disillusionment among its supporters. What began in the 1960s as an effort to create employment and educational opportunities for nonwhites traditionally denied them because of their race or color became increasingly attacked as "reverse discrimination," by means of which more qualified whites were denied jobs, promotions, and other benefits in favor of less qualified nonwhites.

The most thorough recent essay in its defense we have seen is the one we reprint by Burke Marshall and Nicholas deB. Katzenbach. As the headnote to their article suggests (p. 10), they write against a background of firsthand acquaintance with the theory and practice of affirmative action programs from their inception. Among its other values, this essay provides a capsule history of affirmative action (paras. 7–12) and explains why such programs were needed — and are still needed. They also explain some of the key terms in which the controversy over affirmative action is formulated — especially "merit," "preference," "goals," and "color blind."

Conspicuous by its absence in their essay is any mention of *quotas*, the worst aspect of affirmative action according to its critics. Had Katzenbach and Marshall chosen to expand on this concept, they might have said something like the following. First, racial *quotas* — a fixed number or percentage of minority persons to be added to a workforce or other group — are rare. Quotas were introduced into affirmative action programs by the courts in response to the failure of employers and unions to make a good-faith effort to achieve *goals* for minority hires and trainees. Thus quotas have a punitive dimension wholly lacking in goals and were a last resort for failure to make progress toward the goal of a racially integrated workforce.

The case of *Local 28 v. Equal Employment Opportunity Commission* (1986) is one of the most dramatic in which the futile attempt to get a group (in this case a New York City sheet metal union) to remedy its racist practices led to a court-ordered quota of trainees. Local 28's refusal to admit any nonwhites into its membership was so blatant and extensive that it is difficult to imagine anyone familiar with the details of the case concluding that the courts overreached themselves in forcing Local 28 to comply with a quota of minority trainees, a quota that began as a goal.

Critics of affirmative action have often argued that for most practical purposes, racial goals often become de facto quotas. This allegedly happens because employers or unions, afraid that some court will judge them to be not in compliance with their goal, decide on their own to treat that goal as if it were a strict quota. How extensive this tactic has been over the past four decades and how much harm it has caused is undetermined.

Unmentioned by Katzenbach and Marshall in their essay is the important social science research that tends to show that career-enhancing benefits flow from affirmative action college admission programs. This evidence may be found in *The Shape of the River: Long-Term Consequences of Considering Race in College and University Admissions* (1998), by Derek Bok (former president of Harvard) and William G. Bowen (former president of Princeton). The inferences from the data central to the Bok-Bowen research have been challenged in another major treatise on the subject, *American in Black and White*, mentioned earlier.

Where does the nation stand on affirmative action after the latest round of Supreme Court decisions? By way of partial answer, in our casebook on diversity in college admissions in Chapter 3, we reprint excerpts from the two relevant cases that the Court decided in June 2003. In the case of *Grutter v. Bollinger* the Court upheld the use of race in university admissions, provided it was just one of many considerations weighed by the admissions committee, as was the practice in law school admissions at the University of Michigan. We reprint excerpts from the majority opinion for the Court, written by Justice Sandra Day O'Connor. At the same time, however, in the case of *Gratz v. Bollinger* the Court ruled unconstitutional any attempt to treat race as a fixed factor favoring admission to college as was done for freshmen applicants at the University of Michigan. We reprint excerpts from a dissenting opinion by Justice Ruth Bader Ginsburg. Thus the friends and the opponents of affirmative action in higher education have grounds for satisfaction as well as dissatisfaction in these two latest decisions.

2
Cell Phones: Should Their Use While Driving Be Prohibited? (p. 20)

Advocates for Cell Phone Safety

Yes, Prohibit Their Use (p. 20)

We include this pair of essays (this one and the next) for two reasons: (1) The topic is of some significance, and (2) in our view both essays contain some passages of weak writing. The second reason may seem very strange — surely, one might think, the essays in the book ought to be good enough to serve as models — but we think that an occasional weak piece of argument may be useful by providing students with an example of how not to do it.

We don't mean that the writing in these pieces is dreadful, but we do think that if students are invited to study certain paragraphs carefully, they will see that they can improve on them. The lesson ought to be twofold: (1) Just because something has been published does not mean that it is good, and (2) the average student, urged to think about a weak paragraph, can indeed improve it — and thus gain self-confidence.

In the essay by the Advocates for Cell Phone Safety, we wonder about the strategy of beginning with a quotation that states the view that the essay attempts to refute. Generally, an epigraph provides the theme of the essay, and we are inclined to think that the authors made a mistake in giving their opponents' view such prominence. Yes, they go on to try to refute it, but there it is, and a reader who is unconvinced by their statistics may well cling to the idea that indeed "there isn't enough evidence."

Their own comments on statistics are somewhat puzzling. The second paragraph says that we do not have the statistics ("we don't currently collect them"), but their third paragraph gives some figures "assigned" by the Harvard Center for Risk Analysis. We might pause right here and ask ourselves, Are the authors saying that these figures are significant, or are they suggesting (in the word "assigned") that the figures are highly conjectural and therefore not significant? Given what the authors told us in the preceding paragraph ("we don't have statistics"), one can only say that in effect the authors now are saying, "We don't have statistics, but here are figures that one outfit has come up with, on God-only-knows what basis, and we urge you to accept them."

Clearly, the authors want to use these statistics, even though they say that solid statistics are not available. What might they have written? Something like this:

> Although no organization — not the U.S. government, the auto industry, or consumer or safety groups — has collected most of the relevant statistics on the risks of driving while using cell phones, some useful figures are indeed available, and they enable us to make some reasonable conjectures. The National Highway Transportation Safety Administration says. . . .

A statement along these lines presumably is true and in any case would assure the reader that the writers are persons of integrity (a matter of *ethos*). In our view, the original statement tells the reader that the writers are muddle-headed.

As it stands, when a reader of the original essay encounters in the fourth paragraph the statement that "The National Highway Transportation Safety Administration (NHTSA) says that . . . ," the reader is prompted to think, "Wait a minute: 'says that?'" Again, are we getting meaningful figures, or are we getting stuff that people "say," maybe because it is in their interest to say such and such? In short, we think this is a dreadful way to argue. If they want to say that the statistics are uncertain, fine, let them say so, and let them — if they wish to use statistics — then add things like "But the best indications are" and "The most reliable sources say."

The final paragraph of the essay (referred to in our third question) seems to us to make a good point (companies promote safety in the information packet that accompanies the cell phone, but this is to safeguard them against litigation), but curiously the paragraph makes no effort to wrap things up or to bring the essay to a conclusion. Instead of concluding effectively, the essay just stops. The authors might at least have alerted the reader by beginning the paragraph with a signpost such as "Finally" or "Against all such arguments the phone companies can say they have a conclusive response: They. . . . But. . . ." We are certainly not suggesting that the final paragraph should end with "Thus I have proved," or "We have now seen," but we do think that in some way it should wrap things up rather than end with a sentence that explains why the cell phone companies provide literature. The paragraph might at least have ended — here we give one example out of a hundred possible examples — by picking up the word "litigation" (the last word in the present final sentence) and adding

> And there certainly will be plenty of litigation — because there will be plenty of loss of life — if the use of cell phones in automobiles is not regulated.

That's not a great ending, but we think it is an acceptable ending, whereas we think the present ending is unacceptable.

We urge you to ask a student to read the final paragraph aloud in class, invite the class to discuss it, and then ask students to draft a revision. We believe they will enjoy the job of improving on a published essay.

Incidental information: (1) New York has a $100 fine for driving while holding a cell phone to one's ear. Other states are contemplating comparable laws, and perhaps by the time this page is printed, some states will have passed such laws. (2) Opponents to this sort of law argue that other distractions — pushing aside a pet, talking to unruly children in the back seat, drinking a cup of coffee, lighting a cigarette — are equally distracting. (3) We have been told that a study by the *New England Journal of Medicine* of 5,980 Canadian drivers found that the crash risk for drivers using cell phones was four times higher than it was for drivers who were not using cell phones.

Robert W. Hahn and Paul Tetlock

No, Don't Prohibit Their Use (p. 22)

We think that the essay begins engagingly: It lets us hear a driver uttering the opposition view (that drivers who use cell phones can cause accidents). Then, presumably having hooked the audience in the first two paragraphs, in the third paragraph the writers begin to do a U-turn: "But does a ban make sense?" They go on for a moment seeming to advance the no-phone view ("At first blush, it seems a no-brainer if cell phones are indeed causing accidents"), but they promptly go on to point out that *lots* of other activities, including keeping the kids in the back seat quiet, can cause car accidents and that no one proposes regulating such behavior. (A reasonable reply, we think, might be: "Right, we can't possibly pass legislation that will prevent kids from squabbling, so the resultant accidents will indeed happen. But we *can* pass legislation that will reduce accidents due to the use of cell phones, so we ought to do what we can do.")

The argument offered in this essay, as we understand it, depends chiefly on statistics: "While in-car phoning does increase risk, the benefits far outweigh the costs." We then get statistics — from unnamed sources — about the billion-dollar losses in "time and productivity" that would ensue if cell phones were not used in cars. We also get statistics, again from unnamed sources, about how many lives might be saved, and we are told at the end of paragraph 6, "Thus, on balance, the safety purchased with a cell phone ban would simply be too expensive."

We confess that when we first read this essay, with its unsourced statistics and its high valuation on productivity (versus human life), we wondered if it was a spoof: The statistics are so evidently drawn out of thin air, and the tone is so glib. In effect the writers say, "All that loss of productive time and dollars — to save some lives!" Is this the world of "A Modest Proposal"? Look, for instance, at the final paragraph, where the authors suggest that until we get all the figures, "governments should let the 77 million Americans who own cellular phones make their own decisions about when to use them." No one can quarrel with the view that the statistics should be collected. But here we go back to the author's own first paragraph: If we do see that drivers using cell phones are "weaving wildly," well, it may not be enough to say that the people who own cell phones should be left alone to make their own decisions about when to use them.

As we said, for a moment we thought the essay might be a spoof, but these authors are serious, or at least the journal that printed them assumed they are serious because, in a pro/con unit, the journal juxtaposed this essay with the piece arguing on behalf of the ban.

3
Censorship: Should Public Libraries Filter Internet Sites? (p. 24)

David Burt

Yes, Install Filters (p. 25)

The gist of this argument surprised us. We thought the reason for installing filters was to ensure that minors would not have access to pornography. David Burt, however, builds his case on adults who misbehave in the library. Very odd.

The essay presents no difficulties; its rhetorical style also presents little to talk about, although we might ask students what they think of the opening sentence:

> In communities across America, a controversy is raging over how to cope with the problems of library patrons using Internet terminals to access illegal obscenity and child pornography.

Somehow — we hope we don't sound calloused — to our ears "In communities across America, a controversy is raging" sounds a bit too grand, a bit too melodramatic for the fuss about filters in public libraries. But even if this opening sentence is a bit inflated, the piece as a whole is readable, and the final paragraph brings it to a forceful close:

> Public libraries don't stock *Hustler* next to *House & Garden* in their magazine section, so why should they offer Hustler.com? They shouldn't. Not when there is a tested effective solution widely available.

We like the witty juxtaposition of *Hustler* and *House & Garden* (the two magazines probably would indeed be adjacent on shelves where magazines are arranged alphabetically), and we like the short second sentence here — very powerful, we think. And we like the final sentence, with its assertion that a remedy is at hand. The real issue, however, is whether the analogy is valid. True, the library doesn't buy *Hustler*, but as we say in our second question in the text, Supreme Court Justice Souter said the proper analogy is not to the library's unwillingness to buy a publication; rather, he said, the analogy should be to buying a book and then keeping it from the patrons or cutting out objectionable portions.

Analogies are tricky. One hears cries of "False analogy," but *all* analogies are false to some degree. Yes, it is useful to compare X to Y ("We shouldn't change horses in midstream"), but as we say in the text, voters are not riders, and a political crisis or a war is not a stream. The figure is powerful, but what does it prove about voting for the incumbent in a time of crisis? Similarly, it is true that libraries don't stock *Hustler* — by the way, why don't they, since they stock plenty of other material that is frivolous? — but does that prove that libraries *should* block access to Hustler.com on their computers? Burt's short essay, and especially his analogy at the end, ought to provoke good discussion.

Nancy Kranich

No, Do Not Install Filters (p. 26)

Nancy Kranich, unlike Burt, sees the issue as one of protecting children, and she argues — she makes the point clear in her first sentence — that "Filters are neither the best nor the only means to protect children using the Internet in libraries." She builds her case on two points: Filters are not 100 percent safe, and, second, they block "constitutionally protected speech about many subjects people need to know." The Supreme Court has now ruled on this second point, as we say in our headnote.

Kranich is right in saying that the filters do not always block certain kinds of obscene or pornographic material, but it is our understanding that they do indeed block a good deal of such material. She also argues that there are "library policies that address appropriate use and invoke disciplinary action for violators." She doesn't go into detail, and we have no knowledge of such programs, but perhaps your students may know about these things or can learn about them by consulting librarians and can discuss the merits of various programs in class.

Despite the Supreme Court's ruling, we can still discuss the issue, both from a constitutional point of view and from the point of view of protecting children. Let's assume it is agreed that children should not have access to pornographic material. One possible solution — not used, so far as we know — is this: Delegate a batch of computers, with filters, for the use of minors, and prohibit minors from using the other computers. Admittedly, a librarian would occasionally have to ask a young person who was using the computers in the adult room, "May I see your ID?" but would that be unreasonable or unworkable? Just a suggestion.

4
Gay Marriages:
Should They Be Legalized? (p. 29)

The chief arguments, pro and con, seem to be these:

Pro

1. Various human rights acts are violated if gay marriage is denied. For example, in Washington, D.C., the Human Rights Act of 1977 says, "Every individual shall have an equal opportunity . . . to participate in all aspects of life." The choice of one's marital partner is protected by the Constitution, which guarantees each person's right to "life, liberty, and the pursuit of happiness." In pursuing happiness, one ought to be allowed to marry a person whom one loves. It was on this ground that laws forbidding miscegenation were struck down.

2. Marriage gives societal recognition to a relationship.

3. Marriage confers numerous material benefits, such as pensions, health coverage, property rights, even citizenship.

4. Until 1967 interracial marriage was prohibited in about one-third of the states in this country. Opponents of interracial marriage argued, like today's opponents of gay marriage, that it threatened traditional values. We now see that this position was wrong.

5. Marriage — not "civil union" or "domestic partnership" — is what some gays want. They do not wish the sort of "separate but equal" status that "civil union" and "domestic partnership" imply, for such terms in effect stigmatize the relationship as something less than a loving relationship between two human beings. True, they cannot without a third party produce a child — but neither can an infertile or sterile heterosexual couple.

6. The fact that the Bible does not sanction homosexual relationships is irrelevant. In our society, church and state are separate. And if the Bible's view of marriage were relevant, today we would tolerate polygamy and would regard wives as the property of their husbands.

7. Gay marriage promotes fidelity and indeed it promotes family life: Gay couples who adopt children have added incentives to stay together. Further, there is no evidence that children

11

brought up by gays are less stable than children brought up by heterosexuals.

8. Gay marriage does not diminish anyone else's right to marry.

Con

1. It is unnatural, illegal, unsanctioned by the Bible, and a threat to traditional values.

2. Such a marriage cannot produce children, and a marriage that lacks children is especially vulnerable. "Children are the strongest cement of marriage" (Richard A. Posner, *Sex and Reason* [1992], 305). This argument assumes, among other things, that gay persons cannot adopt children or do not have children from a former relationship.

3. If there are children (adopted or from a previous marriage) in a gay marriage, they are at a disadvantage because children need a father and a mother.

4. Males seek variety, and so a union of two men is doubly unstable (Posner says, p. 306, "The male taste for variety in sexual partners makes the prospect for sexual fidelity worse in a homosexual than in a heterosexual marriage").

Although the right to marry is recognized as a fundamental right protected by the due process clause of the Fourteenth Amendment, no state (as of August 2003) recognizes gay marriages. State courts have routinely defined the right as conditional, the right being interpreted as freedom only to enter a heterosexual marriage. This interpretation is based on the traditional view of marriage. It should be mentioned, however, that some states now recognize "domestic partnerships" for same-sex couples, which means that financial benefits (pensions, inheritance, etc.) are available. In 1993, when Hawaii seemed about to recognize marriage (rather than mere "partnership"), other states grew nervous, fearing that they would have to recognize as legitimate a same-sex marriage recognized by Hawaii. In fact, Hawaii's state constitution was amended to exclude gay marriage, but in February 1995 Utah legislators voted to deny recognition to marriages performed elsewhere that do not conform to Utah law. As of 2003, thirty-seven states have officially barred gay marriages. Further, in 1996 President Clinton signed the Defense of Marriage Act, which denies partners in gay marriages federal tax, pension, and other benefits.

Several cities in California, however, have given legal recognition to the "domestic partnership" of homosexual couples and of unmarried heterosexual couples. (We will also see, in a moment, that the New York Court of Appeals — the highest court in the state — ruled in 1988 that a longtime gay union can be regarded as a "family.") For instance,

Berkeley has extended health benefits to the unmarried partners of city workers. In 1989 a law in San Francisco authorized a plan whereby domestic partners are accorded the same hospital visitation rights as are accorded to married couples, and extended to city employees the bereavement leave policy that previously had been limited to married couples. (Cities may extend family benefits to their unmarried employees, but federal law prohibits cities from requiring private companies to do the same.) The San Francisco ordinance defines a domestic partnership as consisting of "two people who have chosen to share one another's lives in an intimate and committed relationship." The two must live together and be jointly responsible for basic living expenses. Neither may be married to anyone else. The couple publicly registers (the fee is $35), in the same way that other couples file for marriage licenses, and the partners must file a notice of termination if their relationship ends. (Roughly speaking, the idea that a gay couple can constitute a family is based on the idea that a family is defined by functions. In 1987 the California State Task Force on the Changing Family, established by the state legislature, said that the functions of the family include maintaining the physical health and the safety of members, providing conditions for emotional growth, helping to shape a "belief system," and encouraging shared responsibility.)

On April 25, 2000, Vermont passed a bill allowing same-sex couples to enter into a "civil union." Civil-union partners are guaranteed various rights in areas of child custody, family leave, inheritance, and insurance.

Canada in 2003 legalized same-sex marriages ("the lawful union of two persons"). There is no residence requirement for a Canadian wedding, so U.S. citizens can go to Canada and get married, but the union is not recognized in the United States for purposes of taxation or immigration.

Here are some figures, as of August 2003:

- A Gallup poll released in late July said that 57 percent of the persons polled opposed gay civil union, *up* from 49 percent in May. (The Supreme Court's decision to strike down a Texas antisodomy law could have increased hostility.)
- Seventy percent of Republican voters and 50 percent of Democratic voters oppose gay unions.
- All of the Democratic candidates for president in 2003 opposed gay marriage, but all supported extending legal rights to gay partners.
- President George W. Bush said he was firmly opposed to using the term *marriage* for same-sex couples, but he added what he thought were reassuring words: "I am mindful that we're all

sinners, . . . and I caution those who may try to take the speck out of their neighbor's eye when they've got a log in their own. I think it's very important for our society to respect each individual, to welcome those with good hearts, to be a welcoming country" (qtd. in the *New York Times*, July 31, 2003, p. A1).

Update: On November 18, 2003, the Massachusetts Supreme Judicial Court (the highest court in the state) ruled four to three that the state's constitution gives gay couples the right to marry, and the court granted the state 180 days to make same-sex marriage possible. Predictably, many legislators began searching for options short of legitimizing gay marriage. The case was brought by fourteen people — seven gay and lesbian couples — who had unsuccessfully sought marriage licenses in various town or city offices in Massachusetts. A lower-court judge had dismissed the case in 2002 on the ground that because same-sex couples cannot have children, the state does not give them the right to marry.

"The question before us," wrote Chief Justice Margaret H. Marshall, "is whether, consistent with the Massachusetts Constitution, the Commonwealth may deny the protections, benefits and obligations conferred by civil marriage to two individuals of the same sex who wish to marry." She went on: "We conclude that it may not. The Massachusetts Constitution affirms the dignity and equality of all individuals. It forbids the creation of second-class citizens."

The ruling provoked strong responses. For instance, Tony Perkins, president of the Family Research Council, said that "it is inexcusable for this court to force the state legislature to 'fix' its state constitution to make it comport with the pro-homosexual agenda of four court justices." He added that the decision shows the need for a federal amendment banning gay marriage: "We must amend the Constitution if we are to stop a tyrannical judiciary from redefining marriage to the point of extinction." President George W. Bush, who opposes same-sex marriage but does not (at the time of this writing, November 2003) favor a constitutional amendment, said, "Marriage is a sacred institution between a man and a woman. Today's decision of the Massachusetts Supreme Judicial Court violates this important principle. I will work with Congressional leaders and others to do what is legally necessary to defend the sanctity of marriage." (qtd. in the *New York Times*, Nov. 19, 2003, p. A19).

In defending the status quo, Massachusetts officials had argued that

1. The main purpose of marriage is procreation,
2. Heterosexual marriage is best for child rearing, and
3. Gay marriage will impose a financial burden on the state.

Chief Justice Marshall dismissed these arguments, saying that the state "failed to identify any constitutionally adequate reason for denying civil marriage to same-sex couples."

By the way, because this case is based in state law, it cannot be appealed to the United States Supreme Court, and it cannot be over-turned by the state legislature. Some experts now say that possibly the legislature might create a relationship that is not called marriage but that does allow for recognition of property rights and joint ownership and child custody, but other experts say that the court's extensive dis-cussion of marriage makes it unlikely that the creation of mere "civil unions" will be satisfactory. The prevailing view seems to be that the only way the state can escape from the court's decision is for the legis-lature to amend the state constitution.

The thirty-four-page ruling asserts that the prohibition against civil marriages for same-sex couples violates the Massachusetts constitu-tion. Following are excerpts from the majority opinion by Chief Justice Marshall. We urge you to consider photocopying these excerpts and inviting students to respond to the arguments.

> The Massachusetts Constitution affirms the dignity and equality of all individuals. It forbids the creation of second-class citizens. In reaching our conclusion, we have given full deference to the arguments made by the Com-monwealth. But it has failed to identify any constitutionally adequate reason for denying civil marriage to same-sex couples.
>
> We are mindful that our decision marks a change in the history of our marriage law. Many people hold deep-seated religious, moral and ethical con-victions that marriage should be limited to the union of one man and one woman and that homosexual conduct is immoral. Many hold equally strong religious, moral and ethical convictions that same-sex couples are entitled to be married and that homosexual persons should be treated no differently than their heterosexual neighbors.
>
> Neither view answers the question before us. Our concern is with the Massachusetts Constitution as a charter of governance for every person prop-erly within its reach. "Our obligation is to define the liberty of all, not to man-date our own moral code." . . .
>
> No one disputes that the plaintiff couples are families, that many are par-ents and that the children they are raising, like all children, need and should have the fullest opportunity to grow up in a secure, protected family unit. Sim-ilarly, no one disputes that, under the rubric of marriage, the state provides a cornucopia of substantial benefits to married parents and their children. The preferential treatment of civil marriage reflects the legislature's conclusion that marriage "is the foremost setting for the education and socialization of chil-dren" precisely because it encourages parents to remain committed to each other and to their children as they grow.
>
> In this case, we are confronted with an entire sizable class of parents rais-ing children who have absolutely no access to civil marriage and its protections

because they are forbidden from procuring a marriage license. It cannot be rational under our laws, and indeed it is not permitted, to penalize children by depriving them of state benefits because the state disapproves of their parents' sexual orientation. . . .

The plaintiffs seek only to be married, not to undermine the institution of civil marriage. They do not want marriage abolished. They do not attack the binary nature of marriage, the consanguinity provisions or any of the other gate-keeping provisions of the marriage licensing law. Recognizing the right of an individual to marry a person of the same sex will not diminish the validity or dignity of opposite-sex marriage, any more than recognizing the right of an individual to marry a person of a different race devalues the marriage of a person who marries someone of her own race.

If anything, extending civil marriage to same-sex couples reinforces the importance of marriage to individuals and communities. That same-sex couples are willing to embrace marriage's solemn obligations of exclusivity, mutual support and commitment to one another is a testament to the enduring place of marriage in our laws and in the human spirit.

Note: In the dissent, Justice Robert Cordy argued that the marriage law was intended to apply to a man and a woman and that "it furthers the legitimate purpose of ensuring, promoting and supporting an optimal social structure for the bearing and raising of children."

Religion and Gay Marriage

Hebrew scripture clearly disapproves, in the strongest terms, of homosexual activity: Leviticus 20: 13, for instance, says, "If a man also lie with mankind, as he lieth with a woman, both of them have committed an abomination: they shall surely be put to death." Persons who today wish to diminish this passage point out that Hebrew Scripture also says, "Thou shalt not wear a garment of divers sorts, as of woolen and linen together" (Deuteronomy 22: 11) and that it prescribes stoning to death for premarital sex and for adultery (Deuteronomy 22: 15–24). To the best of our knowledge, Jesus said nothing about homosexuality, and Paul made a few fleeting references to it.

Given the condemnation in the Bible, where homosexual activity is said to be sinful, and given that "marriage is . . . an honorable estate, instituted of God" (traditional beginning of the Christian wedding liturgy), how can the union of homosexuals be seen as a covenant with God? The chief strategy of those favoring gay marriage has been to point out — as we pointed out in the previous paragraph —that certain other passages describing sinful behavior are no longer heeded.

It is our impression that although many people oppose gay "civil unions," the real trouble comes with gay *marriage*, since for most Americans marriage has religious connotations, and most religious denominations in the United States do not approve of gay marriage. Even the Episcopal Church leaders who in early August 2003 approved the appointment of a gay bishop rejected on the very next day a proposal for blessing same-sex unions. It is commonplace to hear foes of gay marriage say (probably correctly) that all sacred texts of the world's major religions include passages condemning homosexual activity. And even many people who do not regard themselves as very religious nevertheless regard marriage as a religious act and have the ceremony conducted in a church or synagogue.

The Establishment Clause of the First Amendment says we should *not* let religious views determine the laws of the country, but given the widespread sentiment that marriage is a matter of religion, most gay leaders seem to think it is strategically best to focus on the legal aspects of gay unions (such as social security benefits, Medicare, bereavement leave, and authority over funeral decisions), not on the religious implications of gay marriage.

Thomas B. Stoddard

Gay Marriages: Make Them Legal (p. 29)

Thomas B. Stoddard's short essay is interesting in itself, but it may also be used in connection with several of the essays in Chapter 29, What Is the Ideal Society? Paragraph 4, for instance, quotes the Supreme Court's declaration that marriage is "one of the basic civil rights of man." One might also cite *Loving v. Virginia* (1966). ("Loving" is a man, not an action, and "Virginia" is the state, not a woman.) In this case the Supreme Court of the United States held that "the freedom to marry has long been recognized as one of the vital personal rights essential to the orderly pursuit of happiness by free men." (The Court's language is unfortunately sexist, but, as someone has pointed out, in legal language "the male embraces the female.") In the eyes of many, however, homosexuality is a moral disorder, and gay people have no legitimate claim to protection of civil rights. One argument against official attempts to legalize homosexual relations is that the government should seek to treat and rehabilitate homosexuals rather than legitimize homosexuality.

Stoddard begins effectively, we think, first by starting with a cherished quotation and then by showing us that a loving couple was prevented (at least for a while) from living together, "in sickness and in health." His choice of an example — a real example and so not one that can easily be dismissed as far-fetched — is worth discussing in class. He might have chosen two men, one of whom was incapacitated by

AIDS, but he chose two women, one of whom was injured by a drunk driver. First, why women rather than men? It's probably true to say that the general public — and that is the public that Stoddard is addressing in this op-ed piece from the *New York Times* — is less disturbed by two women living together than by two men living together. (The reasons for this difference in attitude are worth thinking about.) Second, by choosing a person who was injured by a drunk driver, he gains the reader's sympathy for the couple and for his own position. The woman is clearly an innocent victim. Not everyone sees a homosexual male with AIDS as an innocent victim.

A second point about the way the essay develops: Stoddard holds off discussing the financial advantages of legalizing gay marriages until his fifth paragraph. That is, he begins by engaging our sympathies, or at least our sentiments, and only after quietly appealing to our emotions does he turn to financial matters. (Marriage of course confers legal, financial, social, and, presumably, psychological benefits.) The financial matters are legitimate concerns, but if he began with them he might seem to be trivializing love and marriage. Stoddard mentions inheritance without a will (this, by the way, is allowed in Sweden), insurance, pension programs, and tax advantages. He omits at least one other important benefit that marriage can confer: A citizen who marries an alien can enable the spouse to become a citizen. (At the end of our discussion of Stoddard's argument we will return to the issue of benefits conferred by marriage.)

Paragraph 6 introduces the point that traditional marriage was often limited to partners of the same race. (Doubtless in this country the aim was to prevent whites and blacks from marrying. Thus, in Virginia the law prohibited Caucasians from marrying non-Caucasians, but it did not care in the least if an African American married a Native American or an Asian. Although the law doubtless was aimed at black-white marriages, it also prohibited Caucasian-Asian marriages. In the 1950s a Caucasian friend of ours who taught in Virginia married a Japanese American woman and therefore had to leave the state or face prison.)

The eighth paragraph addresses what probably is the most common objection to gay marriages: They are antifamily. Stoddard responds by arguing that since marriage "promotes social stability," in our "increasingly loveless world" gay marriages "should be encouraged, not scorned." Moreover, if marriage were only a device to develop families, sterile couples should be refused permission to marry. Since sterile couples are permitted to marry, gays should also be permitted (para. 9). The gist of the idea, thus, is: Marriage is a union of a loving couple; gays can be loving couples; therefore gays should be allowed (legally) to marry. (Here we might add that the view that marriage exists as a protected legal institution primarily to ensure the propagation of the human race, though often stated by the Supreme Court in the past, is no longer strongly held, and many legal scholars doubt that the Supreme Court will in the future take this position. The prevailing view now is that if children are born, they are born as a result of a loving union, but even if no children are born, there remains the loving union.)

The next-to-last paragraph returns to the lesbian couple of the opening. Because students often have trouble ending their essays, we call their attention to the often-used device of tying up the package, at the end, by glancing at the beginning. Of course one can't always finish this way, but it is usually worth thinking about relating the end to the beginning. In any case such thought may stimulate the writer to alter the beginning or to think further about organization. Strictly speaking, Stoddard does not end with Thompson and Kowalski, since he uses them in his penultimate rather than in his final paragraph, but his reference to the couple helps to unite the essay and to bring it to its close.

The final paragraph consists of two sentences, the first essentially a summary (but, mercifully, without such unnecessary words as "Thus we have seen"), the second essentially a vigorous call to justice. Having set forth his argument (with supporting evidence) in previous paragraphs, Stoddard now feels he can call a spade a spade, and he uses stock terms of moral judgment: "fair-minded people" and "monstrous injustice." This last sentence is especially worth discussing in class: Is such language acceptable? That is, has Stoddard earned (so to speak) the right to talk this way, or is the language not much more than hot air? (Our own feeling is this: The essay has made some interesting points, and we understand that the writer now feels entitled to speak rather broadly, but we wish his last sentence were not so familiar.)

Our fifth question asks students to consider whether Stoddard was wise not to introduce the issue of gay couples adopting children. We think he was wise not to get into this issue. Given the fairly widespread belief that gays seduce children and encourage children to become gay, some readers who might be willing to entertain the idea that gays should be able to benefit financially from marriage would draw back from allowing marriage if it meant also allowing gays to adopt children.

Probably similar considerations made it advisable for Stoddard not to enlarge his topic to include polygamy or polyandry. He is not seeking to call into question the whole idea of monogamy, what is sometimes called "natural marriage" (one male and one female); rather, he just wants to enlarge the idea a bit, so that it will accommodate two persons of the same sex. There is no reason, then, for him to ally himself with people whom his readers may consider to be cranks, sex fiends, cultists, and other assorted nuts.

Midway in our discussion of this essay we said that we would comment further on the benefits conferred by marriage. In 1988 a relevant case was decided in New York by the State Court of Appeals. Two gay men in New York City had lived together for more than ten years, sharing a one-bedroom rent-controlled apartment. They had also shared their friends, their business, their checking account, and their vacations. When one of the men died, the landlord sought to evict the survivor. Under rent-control guidelines, a landlord may not evict either "the surviving spouse of the deceased tenant or some other member of the deceased tenant's family who has been living with the tenant." When the issue was first litigated, a lower court decided in favor of the tenant, but the owners of the building appealed, and the Appellate Division in 1988 overthrew the decision. The Appellate Division's ruling held that the tenant's lawyers had not persuasively proved that the legislature intended to give protection under rent-control laws to "nontraditional family relationships." It noted, too, that homosexual couples "cannot yet legally marry," and it said that it was up to the legislature "as a matter of public policy" to grant some form of legal status to a homosexual relationship.

In the appeal the Legal Aid Society spoke of the two men as living in a "loving and committed relationship, functioning in every way as a family." Advocates of the case argued that because the legislature won't act, the courts — though reluctant to make a policy decision by giving gay partners certain legal rights — ought to act. In fact, the court did rule (four to two) that a gay couple could be considered to be a family under New York City's rent-control laws. This decision was the first by a state's highest court to find that a long-term gay relationship qualified as a family. In the majority opinion Judge Vito J. Titone wrote that protection against eviction

> should not rest on fictitious legal distinctions or genetic history, but instead should find its foundation in the reality of family life. . . . In the context of eviction, a more realistic, and certainly equally valid, view of a family includes two adult lifetime partners whose relationship is long-term and characterized by an emotional and financial commitment and interdependence.

The factors that judges and other officials should consider, Judge Titone wrote, include the "exclusivity and longevity" of the relationship, the "level of emotional and financial commitment," the way in which a couple has "conducted their everyday lives and held themselves out to society," and "the reliance placed upon one another for daily family services." Judge Titone's characterization of heterosexual marriage as a "fictitious legal distinction" amazed many observers, who said they might expect such a description from a gay activist but not from a judge.

It is important to realize, however, that the New York decision, which applies also to heterosexuals living together, was narrowly written to deal only with New York City's rent-control regulations. The court avoided ruling on constitutional grounds, which could have opened the possibility of homosexuals qualifying for health insurance benefits normally limited to a spouse or family member.

Stoddard was concerned with this case. When the case was being argued, the *New York Times* quoted him as saying,

> There may be no real alternative to a declaration of new policy from the court. [The court is] dealing with a class of people who are underrepresented in the Legislature, who do not have a strong voice in the democratically elected branches of government and who need the assistance and recognition of the judicial branch to have basic necessities of life preserved for them.

This quotation makes evident a connection between Stoddard's essay and the issue of abortion: Who should decide — the legislatures or the courts? Speaking broadly, the pro-choice people want the courts to decide; they want a ruling that will make unconstitutional the efforts of certain state legislatures to limit abortion. On the other hand, the right-to-life people want the legislatures to be able to establish certain conditions, or limitations. Or put it this way: The right-to-lifers argue that the people (through their elected representatives) ought to make the law; the pro-choicers argue that the courts must act to protect the minority from the tyranny of the majority. Similarly, Stoddard is saying, in the newspaper account, that the judicial branch must come to the aid of underrepresented people. On the other hand, at least in the present climate of opinion, the court might decide that a new definition of marriage is beyond its competence, especially in the absence of any action by the state legislatures showing a willingness to broaden the definition.

A final point: Stoddard does not offer any details about the laws or rituals that might establish gay marriages, but some other advocates have proposed the following:

1. The couple would go to a justice of the peace, who would be authorized by statute to perform the ceremony, or would go to a clergy person.

2. Divorce proceedings would be the same as for heterosexual divorces.

3. A married couple would have all of the financial benefits that are now available to heterosexual married couples.

It may be worth mentioning that it would not follow that homosexual couples would be allowed to adopt children, since in the adoption "the best interest" of the child is the overriding concern. Thus, a legislature might sanction same-sex marriages but might also assert that the psychological climate in such marriages is ill suited to the raising of children. The burden then would be on the couple to prove the contrary. Such legislation would of course not satisfy the gay community.

Lisa Schiffren

Gay Marriage, an Oxymoron (p. 32)

Based on what we have read, it seems to us that most people who favor gay marriage believe that marriage is for love, so gays ought to be allowed to marry, whereas most people who oppose gay marriage say that marriage is for having children (and therefore deserves to be favored by the government), so gays should not be allowed to marry. The view that marriage is for children, not for love, perhaps sounds odd, but probably in the past it was commonplace. Even today it is dominant in some societies (for instance, Japan) where arranged marriages are still not unusual and where many men have mistresses.

If marriage is for children, it makes sense for the government to do what it can to help couples to stay together. But, advocates for gay marriage argue, gays can have children (1) through adoption, (2) through prior marriages, and (3) for lesbian couples, through artificial insemination. Shouldn't the government help such unions to be stable? Conservatives are likely to respond: Most gays do not have children, but even if they do, they ought not to have them because a healthy family normally requires a father and a mother as models of adult male and female behavior.

To the argument that the government helps marriages because it is in society's interest for children to be born into stable relationships, one can respond that some heterosexual couples either cannot have children or do not want to have them, and yet these couples receive the benefits of marriage. If the point of marriage is to establish a stable relationship in which stable children will be reared, why should the government favor the marriage of a sterile couple or of a man to a woman who has passed menopause? Lisa Schiffren faces this issue in paragraph 7, when she says, "Whether homosexual relationships endure is of little concern to society. This is also true of most childless marriages, harsh as it is to say." What answer can be made?

It will be interesting to see what sorts of responses are offered in class. Perhaps some students will argue that an important purpose of marriage — straight or gay — is to *provide sustenance*, to nourish a partner who is ill or depressed, to provide love, if that is not an outdated concept. Of course nothing prevents one person from loving another and providing sustenance in a time of need, married or not, but perhaps marriage — a socially recognized institution — helps a partner to remain a loving partner. The act of taking vows publicly may provide cement in the relationship, and perhaps even persons who are not especially well disposed toward homosexuality may think it is better for there to be homosexual partners than homosexual individuals drifting around.

In paragraph 10 Schiffren turns briefly to the "fairness argument," the argument that the government offers tax advantages and other benefits only to married couples, and homosexuals can't marry. She restates the view that "these financial benefits exist to help couples raise children," but she does not face the question: Why should childless couples also benefit? A possible answer would be that only in the instance of postmenopausal women could one safely predict that the marriage will be childless, and who is going to initiate legislation that will take away benefits from older couples?

NY Times, February 2004

Excerpts from Ruling on Gay Marriage

On February 4, 2004, the Massachusetts Supreme Judicial Court ruled (4–3) that the state must allow gay marriage — not just civil unions — if it is to be in compliance with the Court's earlier ruling in *Goodridge vs. Department of Health*. Here are some excerpts from the ruling of February 4. You may want to photocopy the page and distribute it to students, inviting them to evaluate the arguments.

In *Goodridge* the court was asked to consider the constitutional question "whether the commonwealth may use its formidable regulatory authority to bar same-sex couples from civil marriage." The court has answered the question.

We have now been asked to render an advisory opinion on Senate No. 2175, which creates a new legal status, "civil union," that is purportedly equal to "marriage," yet separate from it. The constitutional difficulty of the proposed civil union bill is evident in its stated purpose to "preserve the traditional, historic nature and meaning of the institution of civil marriage."

Preserving the institution of civil marriage is of course a legislative priority of the highest order, and one to which the justices accord the General Court the greatest deference. We recognize the efforts of the Senate to draft a bill in conformity with the Goodridge opinion. Yet the bill, as we read it, does nothing to "preserve" the civil marriage law, only its constitutional infirmity.

This is not a matter of social policy but of constitutional interpretation. As the court concluded in *Goodridge*, the traditional, historic nature and meaning of civil marriage in Massachusetts is as a wholly secular and dynamic legal institution, the governmental aim of which is to encourage stable adult relationships for the good of the individual and of the community, especially its children. The very nature and purpose of civil marriage, the court concluded, renders unconstitutional any attempt to ban all same-sex couples, as same-sex couples, from entering into civil marriage.

The same defects of rationality evident in the marriage ban considered in *Goodridge* are evident in, if not exaggerated by, Senate No. 2175. Segregating same-sex unions from opposite-sex unions cannot possibly be held rationally to advance or "preserve" what we stated in Goodridge were the commonwealth's legitimate interests in procreation, child rearing and the conservation of resources. Because the proposed law by its express terms forbids same-sex couples entry into civil marriage, it continues to relegate same-sex couples to a different status. The holding in *Goodridge*, by which we are bound, is that group classifications based on unsupportable distinctions, such as that embodied in the proposed bill, are invalid under the Massachusetts Constitution. The history of our nation has demonstrated that separate is seldom, if ever, equal. . . .

The bill's absolute prohibition of the use of the word "marriage" by "spouses" who are the same sex is more than semantic. The dissimilitude between the terms "civil marriage" and "civil union" is not innocuous; it is a considered choice of language that reflects a demonstrable assigning of same-sex, largely homosexual, couples to second-class status. . . .

We are well aware that current federal law prohibits recognition by the federal government of the validity of same-sex marriages legally entered into in any state and that it permits other states to refuse to recognize the validity of such marriages. The argument in the separate opinion that, apart from the legal process, society will still accord a lesser status to those marriages is irrelevant. Courts define what is constitutionally permissible, and the Massachusetts Constitution does not permit this type of labeling.

That there may remain personal residual prejudice against same-sex couples is a proposition all too familiar to other disadvantaged groups. That such prejudice exists is not a reason to insist on less than the Constitution requires. We do not abrogate the fullest measure of protection to which residents of the commonwealth are entitled under the Massachusetts Constitution. Indeed, we would do a grave disservice to every Massachusetts resident, and to our constitutional duty to interpret the law, to conclude that the strong protection of individual rights guaranteed by the Massachusetts Constitution should not be available to their fullest extent in the commonwealth because those rights may not be acknowledged elsewhere. We do not resolve, nor would we attempt to, the consequences of our holding in other jurisdictions. But, as the court held in *Goodridge*, under our federal system of dual sovereignty, and subject to the minimum requirements of the Fourteenth Amendment to the United States Constitution, "each state is free to address difficult issues of individual liberty in the manner its own Constitution demands.

5
Gun Control: Would It Really Help? (p. 36)

Sarah Thompson

Concealed Carry Prevents Violent Crimes (p. 36)

Our uneasiness with statistical evidence is apparent in our discussion of statistics in Chapter 3. We are aware that we are not sophisticated in this area; when we read an argument that uses statistics, we are inclined to say, "Hm, well, that's impressive," but then we read a counterargument, perhaps one that asserts the statistics are flawed because . . . , and we find ourselves agreeing with the counterargument. Further, like most people, we are familiar with a comment that Mark Twain attributed to Disraeli, "There are three kinds of lies: lies, damned lies, and statistics." Jean Baudrillard made a less familiar but equally forceful comment: "Like dreams, statistics are a form of wish fulfillment."

Whatever the merits of her case, we do think Dr. Sarah Thompson is unduly confident about the statistics that she uses. Notice, for instance, that in her final paragraph she says, "In the four years since 1992, those who preach gun control have contributed to the deaths of at least six thousand innocent people." This assertion is probably of a piece with an assertion she rejects in her first paragraph when she says that advocates of gun control claim to have saved 400,000 lives. Probably all such figures are based on dubious extrapolations and can be countered by other figures, equally dubious.

The difficulty of getting useful statistics seems evident to us in Thompson's comment (para. 10) on the Sloan-Kellerman study, which compares Seattle and Vancouver and suggests that gun control laws account for the lower rate of homicide in Vancouver. Thompson says, plausibly, that "There are nearly infinite differences in any two cities," and she goes on to say that "the difference in homicide rates could just as easily have been due to economic, cultural, or ethnic variables, differences in laws, age difference, substance abuse, or anything else." But of course the researchers chose cities that they believed were comparable in significant aspects. In any case, Thompson does *not* specify even one difference that might convince her readers that the cities are not comparable; she merely asserts (as we just heard) that they aren't comparable and that is that. Nevertheless, she says, "As we saw with the Seattle-Vancouver study, if the cities are not well matched, it is easy to draw, or even create, the wrong conclusions" (para. 17). By saying "As we saw," she incorrectly suggests that she actually demonstrated (rather than merely asserted) that Seattle and Vancouver are not well matched. Also worth noting here is her implication that studies comparing cities *can* be valid, if (to use her own words) the cities are "well matched"; she earlier (para. 10) strongly implies that comparisons between cities are pointless because of the innumerable variables.

In our view, Thompson comes across as terrifically eager, deeply sincere, but not a careful thinker and not a particularly effective writer. Her opening paragraph indeed is clear and sets the stage, but as the essay goes on, we think she gets careless. She speaks about "powerful spokespeople" and "doctors and the media" who are recruited to convince the public that guns are bad, but for the most part Thompson does not name names or even give citations of the studies that she angrily dismisses. (You may want some of your students to look at the Sloan-Kellerman study in the *New England Journal of Medicine,* Nov. 10, 1988.)

Notice, too, that although she insists more than once that individuals have a "constitutional right to keep and bear arms" (paras. 37 and 40), she shows no awareness that this right is much disputed. True, the Second Amendment does say "A well regulated militia, being necessary to the security of a free state, the right of the people to keep and bear arms, shall not be infringed." But the meaning of these words is not so clear as Thompson suggests. In 1939 the U.S. Supreme Court held that this amendment guarantees only a collective right for states to arm their militias, and this opinion endured until 1999, when Judge Sam R. Cummings, in a federal Circuit Court of Appeals in Texas, ruled that a citizen has a constitutional right to possess a gun. Several recent books are devoted to interpreting the amendment. Joyce Lee Malcolm, in *To Keep and Bear Arms: The Origins of an Anglo-American Right* (1991), argues that an individual right to weapons goes back to the English Declaration of Rights (1689), which was imported to America and became the Second Amendment. But other scholars say the English Declaration was limited by class and religion and way always subject to regulation. Michael A. Bellesiles, in *Arming America: The Origins of an Anglo-American Right* (1991), argues that contrary to popular belief, in early America few people owned guns, and the drafters of the Second Amendment were *not* thinking about guaranteeing an individual right to guns. Both sides of the controversy invoke Patrick Henry. The pro-gun people call attention to his statement that "The great object is that every man be armed . . . everyone who is able may have a gun." The other side, however, gives the rest of the quotation: "But we have learned, by experience, that, necessary as it is to have arms, and though our Assembly has, by a succession of laws for many years, endeavored to have the militia completely armed, it is still far from being the case. When this power is given up to Congress without limitation or bounds, how will your militia be armed?" That is, the gun-control people say, Patrick Henry was talking about an armed militia, not about the right of an individual to possess a gun.

Back to Thompson's essay, briefly. For obvious reasons she has little to say in response to those persons who call attention to fatal accidents involving guns, especially accidents involving children. As we see it, her first allusion (quite veiled) to the issue is in paragraph 8, where she speaks of people who lose their lives because of "carelessness, or their own stupidity." In paragraph 14 she speaks of "the number of firearm deaths from all causes in a year," a figure that of course includes accidental deaths, but she does not single these deaths out. And in paragraph 23 she says, "In 1993, private citizens accidentally killed 30 innocent people who they thought were committing a crime," but that's about it, so far as the argument goes concerning accidental deaths.

In short, we think Thompson's strength is in her passion; her weakness is in her lack of attention to detail and lack of attention to certain powerful arguments commonly offered by the opposition. And can we say that her final paragraph goes over the top?

> Those who wish to disarm the popular of this country must be exposed for the frauds they are and held responsible morally, if not legally, for the deaths and suffering created by their misguided policies. In the four years since 1992, those who preach gun control have contributed to the deaths of at least six thousand innocent people whose lives they have sworn to protect and whose freedoms they have sworn to uphold.

There is a lot here that one might quarrel with, but we will simply ask, who are these people who have "sworn" to protect others? And is it appropriate to characterize as a "fraud" someone whose policy is "misguided"?

Nan Desuka

Why Handguns Must Be Outlawed (p. 47)

First, a mechanical point that you may wish to mention to students: This essay uses the American Psychological Association (APA) system of documentation.

Nan Desuka denigrates statistics (para. 1) but uses them when they suit her purpose. Probably Desuka's expression of caution about statistics is a way of disarming the opposition because the latter can provide troublesome figures. Moreover, by hinting that the statistics are uncertain and hard to interpret, Desuka presumably implies that the ones *she* offers are reliable and unambiguous. Notice, too, that in her first paragraph she relies on concrete examples — a child or a customer killed accidentally. These examples are the stuff of newspaper accounts, and whatever their statistical probability, we know that such things happen, and so to some extent we are drawn to the author's side.

In the first two paragraphs, largely a warm-up, Desuka seeks to move the reader away from the neat but (she claims) misleading slogans of the gun lobby. Paragraphs 4 and 5, using statistics, are more clearly argumentative. Paragraph 7 advances in some detail a position (handguns should be sold only to police officers) that was briefly introduced in the first sentence of the second paragraph. Notice, too, that this paragraph, like some other passages, conveys a sense of moderation, in order to gain agreement. The author concedes that her proposed solution will not solve the crime problem — but she argues that it will "reduce" crime and that it's a step in the right direction. (Notice, for comparison, that in the next essay the author also makes a concession. This point can be connected to Carl Rogers's essay in Chapter 12.)

In paragraphs 8 and 9 she examines two objections to her proposal, one in each paragraph (cost in dollars and cost in liberty). In the final paragraph she returns to the opening motif of slogans (the tried-and-true formula of ending by echoing the beginning, which is what we are getting at in question 1), and she also repeats the assertion (not really documented in the essay) that handguns usually take the lives of innocent people.

A Note on Statistics and Gun Control

It is hard to know the worth of the statistics that each side regularly produces in this long-running controversy. Take the study with which we are familiar, an article by Arthur Kellermann and Donald Reay in the *New England Journal of Medicine* 314.24 (1986): 1557–60. The authors examined police records of gun-related deaths in King County, Washington (Seattle and surrounding communities), from 1978 to 1983 and found that of 743 deaths, 398 occurred in the home where the weapon was kept. Of these 398, 9 were classified as self-protection, 333 were suicides, 41 were criminal homicides, 12 were accidents, and 3 (all self-inflicted) were of uncertain classification. On the basis of these figures, the researchers argued that a handgun or rifle kept in the home is more likely to kill residents than to protect them. But Paul Blackman, of the National Rifle Association, pointed out that Kellermann and Reay counted only deaths and thus in no way measured, for example, the benefits that accrued when intruders were

(text pp. 36–52)

wounded or frightened away by the use of firearms. Kellermann agreed but countered that the study also omitted nonfatal gunshot injuries of residents in unsuccessful suicide attempts, family arguments, and accidents. The gist of his response is that although the study was limited, a gun in the home probably does more harm than good. Still, one feels the strength of Blackman's point — and one can hardly envision a statistical study that can include a count of crimes *not* committed because the would-be criminal avoids a household that possesses a gun.

Part Two

Casebooks on Contemporary Issues

6
The Death Penalty:
Can It Ever Be Justified? (p. 55)

The continuing salience of the death penalty in our society (as well as the apparent popularity of the topic with users of the book) encourages us again in this edition to devote several essays to the topic. Indeed, we reprint enough material to permit a modest research paper to be written on the strength of this chapter alone. We have kept the debate between former mayor of New York Ed Koch and death penalty attorney David Bruck; two other essays (by Sister Helen Prejean and by Alex Kozinski and Sean Gallagher); and excerpts from the opinions in *Gregg v. Georgia* (1976) and *Callins v. Collins* (1994), two Supreme Court death penalty decisions. We have added a brief and brisk debate between two students over the merits of abolishing the death penalty for juveniles — that is, persons who are under eighteen at the time of the crime (and thus who, virtually without exception, are adults at the time of execution).

As a preface to these essays, here are some basic facts about the death penalty as of summer 2003.

About 3,700 people are currently under sentence of death in thirty-eight states (twelve states have no death penalty), all convicted of some form of criminal homicide. About 18,000 persons are homicide victims each year, about 14,000 persons are convicted of these crimes, and about 300 are sentenced to death. The overwhelming majority of persons on death row are male (nearly 99 percent); about half are white and the rest nonwhite (including about 1,500, or 40 percent, who are African American). In 80 percent of the executions, the murder victim was white.

In the years since 1976, when the Supreme Court validated the constitutionality of the death penalty, 820 persons have been executed. Executions ranged from zero per year in 1978 and 1980 to 25 in 1987 and 98 in 1999. The vast majority have occurred in the South; Texas has executed the most (289) and five states (Colorado, Idaho, New Mexico, Tennessee, Wyoming) have executed but one; nine of the death penalty jurisdictions have executed none. Nine states still use the electric chair, four use the gas chamber, three use hanging, three use the firing squad, and thirty-six use lethal injection; seventeen allow the prisoner to choose between alternatives (for example, hanging or lethal injection).

In recent years, two-thirds of those on death row had a prior felony conviction; 9 percent had a prior conviction of criminal homicide.

The elapsed time between conviction and execution is considerable — ten to fifteen years is not uncommon — owing principally to the appeals taken in state and federal courts. In recent years, roughly 40 percent of all death sentences have been reversed on appeal in federal courts. (It is not known how many are reinstituted by state courts after either retrial or resentencing.)

Our eight excerpts in this chapter do not attempt to present the "human" side of the death penalty — the experiences of the condemned waiting for execution on death row, the frustration inflicted on surviving relatives and friends of the deceased victim by the delays in carrying out the death sentence, the impossible demands made on attorneys on both sides to meet court-imposed deadlines. From among the many books devoted to these aspects of the whole controversy two deserve mention. One is *Dead Man Walking* (1993), by a Roman Catholic nun, Sister Helen Prejean, focusing on her experiences in Louisiana. (We reprint an excerpt from this book, but it is focused on a different aspect of the whole subject.) The film of that title made from her book, available on videocassette, has proved to be a remarkable stimulus to classroom discussion. The other book is *Among the Lowest of the Dead* (1995), by a journalist, David von Drehle, based on his extensive study of Florida's death row prisoners. Neither book is devoted primarily to the argument pro or con, but each adds immeasurably to a better understanding of the impact of the current death penalty system on individual lives.

Elsewhere in the world, according to Amnesty International, seventy-three countries have abolished the death penalty either by law or custom, including all of Western Europe and all the eastern nations that were satellites of the former USSR (except Poland, which has had since 1988 an unofficial moratorium on executions).

Edward I. Koch

Death and Justice: How Capital Punishment Affirms Life (p. 55)

The controversy over the death penalty is a perennial focus of high school debate, and some students will have encountered the issue there. Extensive discussion of almost every claim advanced or contested by Mayor Edward I. Koch and by David Bruck (author of the essay following) can be found in the scholarly literature on the subject; for starters, look at *The Death Penalty in America: Current Controversies* (1997), edited by Hugo Bedau. An unusually extensive exchange in a modified debate format, between John Conrad and Ernest van den Haag, can be found in their book, *The Death Penalty: A Debate* (1983).

Koch opens with several examples that hold our attention. They allow him to get the ironist's advantage by the end of his second paragraph ("their newfound reverence for life"), and they hint at his combative style, which helped make his autobiographical book, *Mayor* (1984), into a best seller.

Koch's essay is a bit unusual among those in the text because he adopts the strategy of advancing his side of the argument by succinctly stating and then criticizing the arguments of the other side. Because he is in control, of course, the other side has to be content with his selection and emphasis; by allowing the other side no more than a one-sentence statement per argument, he makes it look pretty unconvincing.

Koch's concluding paragraphs (15 and 16) are particularly strong because he manages to show his sensitivity to a major claim by the opposition ("the death of . . . even a convicted killer . . . diminishes us all"), even as he implies that the alternative he favors is nevertheless better than the one he opposes. The important details of his own position (question 5) he leaves unspecified.

David Bruck

The Death Penalty (p. 61)

David Bruck's style of argument can be usefully contrasted to Edward I. Koch's. Bruck begins not as Koch did with an example or two (Bruck offers his first example only at para. 4) but with a brief recap of Koch's central position — that morality requires society to execute the convicted murderer. Then, instead of a patient (tedious?) argument-by-argument examination of Koch's position, Bruck tries to make headway by rubbing our noses in some of the disturbing details about the plight of persons on death row that, he implies, cast a different light on the morality of executions.

He then directly challenges (paras. 7–8) one of Koch's principal factual contentions about the possibility of erroneous executions. While we're at it, we can correct Bruck when he writes that Hugo Bedau's research involved about 400 cases "in which the state eventually *admitted* error." The research showed that the state *admitted* error in 309 out of 350 cases — and also that no state has ever admitted executing an innocent person, although Bedau reports that his research shows twenty-three such erroneous executions since 1900. Subsequent to the Koch-Bruck debate, this research has been published in a book, *In Spite of Innocence* (1992), by Michael Radelet, Hugo Bedau, and Constance Putnam.

Worry over convicting the innocent in capital cases reached a new degree of intensity during 2000. In Illinois, prompted by the fact that in recent years as many death row prisoners had been released because of their innocence as had been executed, Governor George Ryan declared a statewide moratorium on executions, to last until he could be assured that effective remedial procedures were in place. Thus Illinois became the first capital punishment jurisdiction to comply with the 1996 recommendation from the House of Delegates of the American Bar Association, urging a nationwide moratorium on the death penalty until procedures were introduced to ensure fairness, due process, and competent counsel for capital defendants. Much of the background to Governor Ryan's decision is discussed in the recent book *Actual Innocence* (2000) by Barry Scheck, Peter Neufeld, and Jim Dwyer. They relate the stories of recent cases (many, but not all, of them involving the use of DNA evidence to exonerate the innocent) that show just how easy it is for the innocent to be convicted and sentenced to death.

In the Koch-Bruck debate, the mayor had the last word, although we didn't reprint it in the text. His objections to Bruck's rebuttal may be found in *The New Republic* (May 20, 1985, p. 21). The main assertion in Koch's response is that "a truly civilized society need not shrink from imposing capital punishment as long as its procedures for determining guilt and passing sentence are constitutional and just." The reader of Koch's original article may well wonder where in it he succeeded in showing that these "procedures" in our society, as actually administered, are "just."

A word about question 4, on the polygraph or "lie detector." The so-called lie detector does not, of course, detect lies. It records physiological phenomena such as abnormal heart beat that are commonly associated with lying. Opponents say it is based on the premise that there is a "Pinocchio effect," a bodily response unique to lying. Opponents of the polygraph argue that the effects recorded, such as an increased heart rate or blood presence, can have other causes. That is, these changes may reflect personal anxieties apart from lying, and, on the other hand, the symptoms may be suppressed by persons who in fact are lying. Wu-Tai Chin, the CIA employee who spied for China for thirty years, "passed" polygraph tests many times. The American Psychological Association, after a two-year study, concluded flatly that polygraph tests are "unsatisfactory." It is also noteworthy that findings from polygraphs are not admitted as evidence in federal courts.

Potter Stewart

Gregg v. Georgia *(p. 66)*

In this case, Justice Brennan and Justice Marshall were the sole dissenters (as they were to be, until their retirement in every death penalty case where the majority upheld the conviction and the sentence).

Question 2 requires the reader to make a sharp distinction between the normative principles asserted by Brennan in *Furman* and the factual claims about the death penalty (its affront to human dignity, its needless severity, and so on) on which Brennan relied. Theoretically, Justice Potter Stewart or anyone else who disagrees with Brennan could do so in any of the following ways: One could (1) reject both Brennan's four principles and his factual claims about the death penalty, (2) reject the principles but agree on the facts, or (3) accept the principles but reject the factual claims. As we examine Justice Stewart's opinion, although he never mentions Justice Brennan by name, we think alternative (1) most nearly describes his position: Stewart does not reject all of Brennan's principles, nor does he reject all of Brennan's factual claims, but he does reject some of both.

As to question 3, it is perhaps worth noting that the House of Delegates of the American Bar Association, meeting in Houston in early 1997, urged a national moratorium on the death penalty until such time as trial and appellate procedures in death penalty cases could be brought into conformity with the requirements of due process of law. For the considerations that lie behind the ABA's position, see *The Death Penalty in America: Current Controversies*, ed. Hugo A. Bedau (1997). It might also be noted that for the first time in over three decades, not a single member of the current Supreme Court is on record as being opposed to the death penalty on constitutional grounds.

Regarding the mandatory death penalty ruled unconstitutional in *Woodson v. North Carolina* (1976) (see question 5), the Court argued that such penalties had been all but completely rejected as "unduly harsh and unworkably rigid" and that they fail "to allow the particularized consideration of relevant aspects of the character and record of each convicted defendant." A decade later, in *Sumner v. Shuman* (1987), the Court went so far as to rule that a mandatory death penalty even for a convicted murderer who murdered again while in prison under a life sentence was unconstitutional.

In discussing question 7, it should be noted that when Congress enacted the Violent Crime Control and Law Enforcement Act of 1994 and the Anti-Terrorism and Effective Death Penalty Act of 1996, the death penalty was authorized for several nonhomicidal crimes. As of 2000, however, the Supreme Court has not ruled on the constitutionality of such punishments.

Harry Blackmun

Dissenting Opinion in Callins v. Collins *(p. 75)*

Justice Harry Blackmun (who died in 1998) had an unusual judicial career where the death penalty is concerned. In the mid-1960s, in the Arkansas case of *Maxwell v. Bishop* (Maxwell was an African American sentenced to death for the rape of a white woman), Blackmun upheld the conviction and sentence in his role as a U.S. Court of Appeals judge. Appointed to the U.S. Supreme Court in 1970, he rendered a tortured dissenting opinion in the *Furman* case two years later, as he struggled unsuccessfully to resolve the tension between his personal opposition to the death penalty and his inability to find a convincing constitutional argument to support that opinion.

After more than two decades on the Court, during which time he confronted scores of capital cases, he emerged toward the end of his life as a staunch opponent of the death penalty, for reasons he explains in his dissent in the *Callins* case of 1994, which we reprint. Paramount in his thinking was the failure of what he called "the machinery of death" — a failure of the criminal justice system compounded out of the racial discrimination and arbitrariness of the decision making in capital cases, faults supposedly cured years earlier by the "new" capital statutes enacted in many states after *Furman*.

Blackmun's dissent is characteristic of most contemporary opposition to the death penalty in America. The focus is on the death penalty *as administered*, not on the death penalty as an abstract matter of right or wrong or even as an unconstitutional "cruel and unusual punishment." It is this emphasis on "the machinery of death" that prompted the American Bar Association's House of Delegates in 1997 to call for a nationwide moratorium on executions until the malfunctioning "machinery" could be repaired. The first such moratorium took effect in Illinois in 2000. In 2003 the Ryan Commission tendered its report, and the immediate result was the governor's decision to cancel all of Illinois's death sentences in favor of pardons for four prisoners and resentencing to life in prison for 163 other prisoners. How many of the Commission's several dozen recommendations will be enacted into law remains to be seen. Whether other states will follow the lead of Illinois is too early to say.

Friends of the death penalty have replied to the kind of argument that Justice Blackmun relies on by insisting that in theory the death penalty can be freed of its current faults, such as they are, and it is the faults, not the death penalty as such, that ought to be abolished. Until they are, the death penalty as such cannot be repudiated as a violation of "equal protection of the laws," of "due process of law," or of any other constitutional principle. Students ought to try to discuss what to make of this reply to Blackmun.

Helen Prejean

Executions Are Too Costly — Morally (p. 80)

Sister Helen Prejean has proved to be the most influential figure — speaker, lobbyist, film consultant, writer, and spiritual adviser to men on death row — currently opposing the death penalty in the United States. Her humor, warmth, and compassion have been much admired, and she has earned the respect of many whose lives have been ravaged by the murder of a loved one — whether in a crime of homicide or in a legally authorized execution. She has brought to the public debate a down-home human approach noticeably absent from much of the discourse on this subject.

The excerpt we reprint from her popular book *Dead Man Walking* is devoted largely to examining the biblical support for (or opposition to) capital punishment. She neglects to mention what many think is the best single passage in the Bible on this subject, Genesis 4: 9–16 — God's response to Cain for murdering his brother, Abel. God punishes Cain in three ways: He is exiled, he is cursed, and he is stigmatized (so that others will recognize him for the murderer he is). Perhaps no other passage in the Bible so personalizes God's punishment meted out to a murderer — not perhaps a perfect paradigm for how today's opponents of the death penalty would have murderers punished but worthy of their thoughtful reflection.

The Judeo-Christian posture on the death penalty is a long story. A small fraction of it is related in paragraphs 11 through 15. Those who seek more must consult the hefty recent monograph by James J. Megivern, *The Death Penalty: An Historical and Theological Survey* (1997). Professor Megivern explains how the Christian church at the time of the First Crusade (1095) abandoned its early commitment to pacifism in favor of Christian triumphalism with sword in hand, led by Pope Gregory VII (1073–1085), his successor Pope Urban II

(1042–1099), and St. Bernard of Clairvaux (1090–1153). Their enemies were infidels (read Jews and Moslems) and soon thereafter Christian heretics. According to Megivern, the epitome of this transformation in the Christian ethic of war and peace, of violence and pacifism, appears in the *Chanson d'Antioche*, "the greatest of the vernacular epics of the First Crusade." Christ is portrayed as hanging on the cross and assuring the good thief to his side that "from over the seas will come a new race which will take *revenge* on the death of the father." Thus, as Megivern notes, was brought to pass a "total reversal of the actual teachings of Jesus."

Casey Johnson and Emma Welch

Should the Death Penalty Apply to Juveniles? (pp. 85, 86)

These brief pro and con essays by teenagers are not models of incisive argument, but they have the merit (we think) of addressing the issue of the death penalty in a manner that most other teenagers would find appropriate and convincing. If your students are somewhat more sophisticated than the average, you should have no trouble in finding a good deal to criticize in each essay.

Let's take a closer look at the legal status of executing juveniles. In 1988, in the case of *Thompson v. Oklahoma*, 487 U.S. 815, the U.S. Supreme Court ruled that execution of an offender fifteen or younger at the time of the crime was unconstitutional. A year later, the Court ruled that the Eighth Amendment (forbidding "cruel and unusual punishments") does not prohibit the death penalty for crimes committed at age sixteen or seventeen (see *Stanford v. Kentucky*, 492 U.S. 361). We choose to reprint this short debate in part because it is possible that in the near future the Supreme Court will decide to reexamine the constitutionality of such executions. Juvenile murderers are the one salient category of offenders today whose exclusion from the death sentence is within the realm of possibility, now that the Court has ruled in 2003 that convicted murderers who suffer from mental retardation are to be exempt from the death sentence.

According to the U.S. Department of Justice, no one seventeen or younger was on death row at the end of 2001, although seventy-seven persons seventeen or younger had been arrested for a capital crime. Between 1973 and 1997, 160 death sentences in twenty-two jurisdictions were issued to youths fifteen to seventeen years of age. This is a small fraction of the over six thousand total death sentences for those years.

According to the same source, seventeen states permit the execution of an offender who is under eighteen but over fifteen. Seven states impose no age limits on eligibility for a death sentence.

International law (to be more precise, the International Covenant on Civil and Political Rights, Article 6, para. 5) declares that "Sentence of death shall not be imposed for crimes committed by persons below eighteen years of age." Our government, however, has signed this Covenant with a reservation of noncompliance with this section. The matter is discussed in considerable detail by William A. Schabas in his masterful treatise, *The Abolition of the Death Penalty in International Law*, 2nd ed. (Cambridge: Cambridge University Press, 1997).

Execution of juveniles is not unknown in other countries. During the 1990s, youths age thirteen to seventeen were executed in Bangladesh, Iran, Iraq, Nigeria, Pakistan, Saudi Arabia, and Yemen.

The most authoritative discussion of the subject is by Victor L. Streib, *Death Penalty for Juveniles* (Bloomington: Indiana University Press, 1987). See also Shirley Dicks, ed., *Young Blood: Juvenile Justice and the Death Penalty* (Amherst, N.Y.: Prometheus Books, 1995).

Alex Kozinski and Sean Gallagher

For an Honest Death Penalty (p. 88)

Judge Alex Kozinski (often mentioned as a possible future Justice of the U.S. Supreme Court) and his junior colleague, Sean Gallagher, advance a line of argument that tries to carve a middle way between outright across-the-board abolition of the death penalty, at the one extreme, and, at the other extreme, the haphazard system that Justice Blackmun has so vigorously criticized elsewhere (see his dissenting opinion in *Callins v. Collins*, reprinted on p. 98 and written about the same time as the Kozinski and Gallagher essay). This is their "political solution" (see question 8) to the death penalty controversy.

Note the world-weary tone in which they write. Kozinski and Gallagher find no merit in any of the standard arguments against the death penalty (see especially paras. 11–12), although they ignore the question of deterrence (and thus we don't know quite what they think of that argument). They seem to rest their case for the Death Penalty Lite on the proposition that the great majority of the public wants it (para. 1) and the public is right: "premeditated murder[ers] justly forfeit the right to their own life" (para. 12). What seems to exercise them is mainly the cost and inefficiency of the present death penalty system; they profess no deep concerns over the morality of that system.

We have to confess some doubt whether their goal of reserving the death penalty "for only the most heinous criminals" (para. 20) is really within reach. When the post-Furman death penalty statutes were enacted in the mid-1970s, their proponents strongly believed that this is exactly what these statutes would do: They had narrowed the death penalty so that it reached only the worst among the bad. But Kozinski and Gallagher fully concede that this effort has proved to be a failure. One really must wonder, therefore, whether it is within the wisdom of any legislature to craft narrow death penalty statutes that will reach only "the most heinous criminals" so long as lay juries have the final decision in applying these statutes. Those who agree with Kozinski and Gallagher might well ponder the words of a much-respected Supreme Court Justice, John Marshall Harlan (not an avowed opponent of the death penalty by any means). In 1971 he wrote: "To identify before the fact those characteristics of criminal homicide and their perpetrators which call for the death penalty, and to express these characteristics in language which can be fairly understood and applied by the sentencing authority, appear to be tasks which are beyond present human ability."

7
Drugs: Should Their Sale and Use Be Legalized? (p. 94)

Next to AIDS, drugs — their use and abuse and the costs of the efforts to control them — may well be the nation's most publicized if not its most pressing social problem. Unlike AIDS, however, drug use leaves few of the users dead; and many of those who do die from drugs do not do so from overdosing or suicide but from shoot-outs in turf wars and busted deals. The four essays we present take several divergent views of the problem and its solution.

In his inaugural address early in 1989, President Bush reassured the nation by declaring "This scourge will end." A few months later, in a special broadcast on the drug problem, he reported that although "23 million Americans were using drugs" regularly in 1985, that number had dropped in 1988 by "almost 9 million." The president credited this gain to his administration's four-point campaign: tougher penalties, more effective enforcement, expanded treatment programs, and education to reach the young who have not yet started to use drugs. An enthusiastic elaboration of the government's efforts is presented in the articles we reprint by William J. Bennett, the nation's first drug czar (a good guy, not to be confused with a "drug kingpin," who is a bad guy) and by James Q. Wilson.

Others are more skeptical. Here are some of the disturbing facts reported in a review article, "What Ever Happened to the 'War on Drugs'?" by Michael Massing in the June 11, 1992, issue of *New York Review of Books*.

How many people are using illegal drugs and how frequently? According to a 1990 household survey reported by the National Institute of Drug Abuse, some 12.9 million of us used such drugs within a month prior to the survey, 11 percent fewer than in 1988 (these figures do not quite jibe with those reported by President Bush). More frequent (weekly) users dropped by 23 percent, from 862,000 in 1988 to 662,000 in 1990. Among adolescents, cocaine use had dropped almost by half. But in 1991, the same agency reported that monthly users of cocaine had jumped 18 percent over 1990, to 1.9 million people. Weekly users had also increased, back to 1988 levels. Emergency hospital visits from cocaine abuse had risen 30 percent over 1990. And heroin was making a return engagement. But casual use of drugs among the middle class continued its steady decline from the mid-1980s. Does all this sound like we are winning or losing the war on drugs?

What about treatment for those who want to shake the drug habit? During President Reagan's first term (again relying on data provided by Michael Massing in his survey), funds for treatment centers (adjusted for inflation) dropped by nearly 40 percent. During Reagan's second term, when crack cocaine reached epidemic proportions in the nation's inner cities, treatment centers were overwhelmed. Both the numbers of those seeking help and the extent of the treatment they needed had grown enormously. With the cocaine-related death of college basketball star Len Bias fresh on everyone's mind, the Bush administration approved a budget of $1.6 billion for treatment centers run by the states, an increase of 50 percent over the funds provided by his predecessor. But even this increase failed to meet the demand for treatment.

Turning from the issues of salience and success in the war on drugs, what is it costing us? In a 1990 article by Ethan Nadelmann, "Should Some Illegal Drugs Be Legalized?" in *Issues in Science and Technology*, we are told that the nation spent $10 billion to enforce our drug laws in 1987, perhaps twice that amount in 1990. Between 40 percent and 50 percent of all felony convictions are for drug offenses. In 1989 alone, "between three-quarters of a million and a million people were arrested . . . on drug charges." To this we must add the indirect costs. International enforcement, interdiction, and domestic enforcement — all essential elements in the government's strategy — have yet to succeed. To put it simply, we need to keep two things in mind. First, we have so far failed to keep drugs from being brought into the country. All the drugs illegal in this country and in wide use nevertheless (opium and heroin, cannabis, coca and cocaine) are native to many foreign countries and are a major cash crop in much of the world. Second, we have not succeeded in drying up demand despite granting substantial resources to law enforcement to do so.

Literature on the drug problem continues to roll off the presses; of the five books in Massing's review survey, we recommend especially *The Search for Rational Drug Control*, by Franklin E. Zimring and Gordon Hawkins, an author team highly regarded for their shelf of books on virtually every problem in criminal justice.

William J. Bennett

Drug Policy and the Intellectuals (p. 94)

William J. Bennett gives a vigorous defense of the national drug policy he was assigned to carry out by the Bush administration. He attacks intellectuals (the only two he names are the liberal columnist Anthony Lewis and the conservative spokesman William F. Buckley Jr.

in para. 8; but he alludes to a host of unnamed "prominent residents" on the campuses of Princeton, Wisconsin, Harvard, and Stanford in para. 18) for their faults in blinding themselves and the nation to the evils of legalizing drug use, a policy supported (he says) by "a series of superficial and even disingenuous ideas" (para. 8).

Here's a quick summary of Bennett's seven-point argument against the legalization of drugs (question 3): (1) criminalizing drugs provides an incentive to stay out of the business (para. 10); (2) no one has figured out how to carry out a policy of legalization of drugs across the board, from marijuana to PCP (para. 11); (3) if drugs are legalized, their use will "soar" (para. 13), thereby increasing the harm and suffering to the users; (4) the cost to the nation of more drug use would be "intolerably high" (para. 14); (5) drug-related crimes would not decrease at all (para. 15); (6) the terrible problems we have with legalized alcohol are a foretaste of the even graver problems we would have were all drugs legalized (para. 16); (7) apart from all the foregoing, "heavy drug use destroys character," "dignity and autonomy" (para. 17). We have to admit Bennett makes a pretty convincing argument, spiced with barbs at "America's pundits and academic cynics" along the way.

Were someone to accuse Bennett of hypocrisy or inconsistency (question 4), he might well reply in the same manner that he does regarding legalization of alcohol (para. 16): No doubt it would be a futile effort for society now to make tobacco use illegal; yet he would be better off (as he might well admit) if he had never acquired the nicotine habit and if he could get rid of it. But whether he can is his personal medical problem; there is no inconsistency in his urging a policy to the effect that everyone (himself included) avoid harmful illegal drugs, even if he is unable to cease using a harmful legal drug himself. Of course, he might also take another line, that nicotine addiction is not as harmful as addiction to any illegal drug. But that is an empirical claim, and it is far from clear whether it is true.

James Q. Wilson

Against the Legalization of Drugs (p. 102)

This essay following William J. Bennett's reminds us of the "good cop/bad cop" routine in police interrogation. We debated whether to include both these essays, since the argument in each is pretty much the same. But the tone is so different — James Q. Wilson thoughtful and patient, Bennett using words as though they were clubs — that we thought this difference itself is worth some reflection. (Students might well be set the task of reading these two essays as a pair and explaining what, if anything, is different in the two arguments and, that apart, which essay has the more persuasive, effective tone.)

The idea of "victimless crimes" (our question 1) gained prominence in the 1960s, as part of an argument for decriminalizing various drug and sex offenses, as well as gambling. When consenting adults engage in illegal practices that harm no one (or harm only themselves), so the argument went, they have committed a victimless crime. But such acts ought to be decriminalized because the criminal law in such cases is improperly invading privacy, liberty, and autonomy. (John Stuart Mill made this argument famous, although he did not use the term *victimless crimes*.) Wilson seems to object to this argument on two grounds (para. 24). First, he rejects the criterion of state intervention as too narrow: "Society is not and could never be," he says, "a collection of autonomous individuals." So we need the criminal law here and there for admittedly paternalistic purposes. Consequently, even if drug abuse were a victimless crime, Wilson might not approve of its legalization. Second, he rejects the factual minor premise of the victimless crime argument; drug use is harmful not only to the user but to others who have not or cannot consent (there is "fetal drug syndrome," for example).

Wilson is a skillful, polished arguer, and we draw attention to some of these features of his essay in two of our questions (the second and the fourth). The "economic dilemma" that the drug legalizers face, to which Wilson refers in his paragraph 37 (our fourth question), can be formulated somewhat more briefly than he does, as follows: Tax money from legalized drugs will pay for the cost of regulation and treatment of users, abusers, and addicts, or it will not. If it does, then the tax rate on drugs must be set quite high; but this will lead to tax evasion and crime and a black market in drugs. If tax money from drugs does not fully finance the costs of regulation and treatment, then we will have more addicts and either inadequately financed treatment centers or less tax money for other public needs. But none of these alternatives is acceptable. Therefore, we cannot reasonably legalize drugs in the expectation that taxing them (as alcohol and tobacco are now taxed) will enable society to pay for the costs.

Like any dilemma worthy of the name (see our discussion of the dilemma in the text), this one has a disjunctive tautology as its major premise (that is, the premise states two exhaustive and exclusive alternatives). Such a premise is invulnerable to criticism. Criticism can be directed, however, at each of the two other conditional premises ("if . . . , then . . ."), as they are empirical generalizations and vulnerable on factual grounds. Or criticism can be focused on the premise that expresses how unacceptable the dilemma is. Perhaps one of these alternatives is not so bad after all, especially when compared with the costs of losing the war on drugs. One way to develop that thought would be by constructing a counterdilemma, showing the awkward consequences of *not* legalizing drugs. (Here, we leave that task for another day.)

In his criticism of Nadelmann (paras. 25–26), Wilson accuses him of "a logical fallacy and a factual error." The fallacy is to infer (1) the percentage of occasional cocaine users who become "binge users" when the drug is *legal* from (2) the percentage who become "binge users" when (as at present) the drug is *illegal*. Why does Wilson think this is a fallacy? To be sure, (1) and (2) are quite independent propositions, and it is possible that the percentage of users would grow (rather than stay roughly constant, as Nadelmann infers) as soon as the drug is legalized. But by how much? At what rate? In the face of antidrug education? These unanswered questions apart, what Wilson needs to show us is that in general, or perhaps in some closely parallel case, the number of those who do X when doing X is illegal has no relationship to the number of those who do X when doing X is legal. But Wilson hasn't shown this at all.

As for the "factual error," it looks to us as though Wilson has caught Nadelmann in an error (see para. 27).

Milton Friedman

There's No Justice in the War on Drugs (p. 117)

Milton Friedman is the nation's best-known free-market economist and the author of many books, including *Capitalism and Freedom* (1962). He and his fellow conservatives seem to be divided over the nation's "War on drugs." Some, like William J. Bennett, strongly favor fighting the use of illegal drugs with unrelenting fervor. Others, believing that drug use harms only or principally the user, oppose government interference (either in the form of regulation or outright prohibition) and favor using free-market methods to control its use. Friedman is of the latter persuasion. He hints at reasons of this sort in his paragraph 2, where he quotes himself from 1972. There, in a phrase, his position was this: Persuasion, yes; coercion, no.

What is surprising about Friedman's essay is that he does not rely on free-market reasoning. It's not that he rejects such reasoning; it's rather that he invokes what he describes as "ethical" considerations of several different sorts. They constitute a variety of objections, each of which represents one kind of empirical consequence of the policy of the past quarter century but inadequately foreseen when the war on drugs was launched with much fanfare by President Nixon in 1972.

Regarding question 1, here is one way the thesis of his essay might be stated in a sentence: "The unethical consequences of the nation's war on drugs far outweigh whatever advantages have been or might be gained." (This version is inspired by the rhetorical question Friedman asks at the end of his essay, in para. 13.)

As to question 2 (and also question 4), an "expediential" objection to the war on drugs would be any claim that its harmful consequences (for example, in tempting the police into corruption) outweigh its good consequences. A moral (or ethical) objection would be that our drug policies violate some moral norm, standard, or principle (for example, the principle that adults ought to be left free of governmental interference to act as they wish — including using drugs — so long as they do not harm others).

Elliott Currie

Toward a Policy on Drugs (p. 120)

Elliott Currie's position on the drug controversy (our question 4) includes three steps: (1) move toward decriminalizing the drug user (but not necessarily the trafficker), (2) treat marijuana (use as well as dealing?) "differently" from (he means more leniently than) "the harder drugs" (mainly heroin and cocaine, we surmise), and (3) permit medical experimentation with certain drugs (which ones he does not say, but marijuana is the obvious example) (para. 18). These recommendations (all adopted in one way or another, he says, by "some European countries") fall well short of radical decriminalization of drugs, but if Currie is right, to go any further is to cause predictable costs and harms that make radical decriminalization the wrong social policy.

Is Currie convincing that these steps, and these only, are a reasonable compromise between those who want to carry on the "war on drugs" no matter what the costs and those who want all aspects of drug use, sale, and manufacture to be permitted by law? (He presented these views nearly a decade ago, and we suspect he would say today that precious little progress has been made over this period to bring any of these three recommendations to come to pass.) We do not have a better proposal to offer, and we think at the very least that his middle way between the two extremes deserves careful thought. The prospect of ideas such as his receiving careful thought at the highest levels in our governments, state and federal, is not encouraging.

In our question 2 we mention three possible steps to reduce the role of drugs in our lives, steps Currie does not mention. Why doesn't he? As a guess, we suggest this. He would reject our first suggestion (curbing manufacture of illegal drugs) because either most of the drugs in question are not manufactured in the United States or the one that mainly is (marijuana) he wants largely to decriminalize. Perhaps he would reject our second suggestion (reducing imports of illegal drugs) on the grounds that federal agencies have tried for years to do precisely this but to little effect and that tax dollars to curb heavy drug importing can be more effectively spent elsewhere. As for our third suggestion (aggressive public education), perhaps he could argue it is implicit and is presupposed in much of what he says.

The evident uniqueness of the magnitude of the drug problem in this country troubles us. Currie mentions the issue (para. 21), but he offers no explanation for our unfortunate plight. We mention (question 5) three possible explanations that seem to us unconvincing. We don't have a fourth to offer for contemplation. So long as there is no convincing and generally accepted explanation, it seems likely to us that the drug problem will not abate. Meanwhile, the human cost in our drug policies ought to terrify and infuriate. In New York, for example, drug laws enacted during the Rockefeller administration (as reported by the Fortune Society) mandate a fifteen-years-to-life sentence for the sale of two ounces or the possession of four ounces of an illegal drug. Is there any convincing reason why our society ought to persist in enacting and enforcing such laws? We earnestly doubt it.

8
The Just War: What Are the Criteria? (p. 132)

Many of the basic ideas of a just war we owe to early medieval Christian thinkers, notably St. Augustine of Hippo (A.D. 354–430). Augustine's ideas include (1) avoiding disproportionate destructiveness in the means of warfare given the ends sought and (2) respecting the immunity of noncombatants. Both of these principles derive from a more fundamental principle of humanity. The enemy soldier is, after all, *human*. Augustine also defended three other relevant principles:

- There must be a just cause for war.
- The war must be authorized by legitimate authority.
- The war must be undertaken with the right intention.

Over the centuries these and other principles emerged that expressed moral limitations on the occasions for and the conduct of war. By the time of Hugo Grotius (1583–1645) many of these principles were incorporated into the emerging natural law of international relations, culminating in the several Geneva conventions adopted early in the twentieth century and in the principles laid down in the post–World War II Nuremberg trials of the major Nazi war criminals.

Worries over whether the war in question was just and was being fought only with just means did not much distress the victors in World War II (but see below in this manual's discussion of G. E. M. Anscombe regarding *jus in bello*) or the Korean War. The Vietnam War of the 1960s was another matter altogether, and an unprecedented interest in the concept of just war was provoked by American intervention and by the tactics and weaponry we used. By the end of the twentieth century it had become commonplace for American critics of our quasi-imperial conduct to evaluate all our military practices from the moral perspective afforded by the criteria of just war. Such critics had a field day in their evaluation of the American invasion of Iraq in March 2003. The heart of the controversy is whether preemptive war (which is what we have in Iraq, according to our government) can be justified by just-war criteria and if it cannot whether that marks a fundamental defect in the use of just-war criteria for evaluating modern warfare.

G. E. M. Anscombe

The Criteria of a Just War (p. 132)

We reprint this short excerpt from a 1939 prewar essay of the youthful Gertrude Elizabeth Margaret Anscombe (1919–2001) because it is the briefest and most accurate statement of the criteria of a just war that we have seen. Notice that we can easily reconceptualize the seven conditions in her definition as follows:

A war is just if and only if . . .

Or we could state it this way:

The sufficient and necessary conditions of a just war are . . .

Notice too that Anscombe does not use the conventional distinction between *jus ad bellum* (the moral criteria for going to war in the first place) and *jus in bello* (the moral criteria for conducting warfare). These are two quite different issues. In theory, one could have a just cause for going to war but then carry out the warfare by unjust means. (Both the British and the American aerial bombing campaign against Germany and Japan, respectively, during World War II have been widely evaluated in precisely this manner.) Conversely, one could have no just cause for war yet carry on a war using only just means — no doubt an unlikely possibility, but possible nonetheless.

To use just-war criteria, it is not enough to agree on the principles, such as those Anscombe specifies. Each of her seven principles depends on factual judgments, most of which are controversial, that must be made before we can conclude that the war is unjust in this or that respect. We leave it up to you and your students to decide as best you can what the facts are and what conclusions they entail as to the justice of the American invasion of Iraq.

Peter Steinfels

The Just War Tradition and the Invasion of Iraq (p. 133)

Peter Steinfels devotes most of his space to discussing one of the several criteria for a just war — namely, that the recourse to war must be the "last resort." He points out how elusive this criterion is: "the last resort is always just over the horizon" (para. 5). (Here we are reminded of a similar criterion usually invoked as a necessary condition of justified civil disobedience — namely, that the dissenters have exhausted all available legal means of protest. What counts as "exhaust" here is akin to what counts as the "last resort.") As to whether our government turned to war in Iraq as a last resort, we do not attempt to decide that issue and leave it for class discussion. Hawks and doves must try to reach agreement on the relevant facts. Where they cannot agree, they must agree to disagree and to that extent leave the fundamental question unanswered. As for Steinfels's own position on the last-resort issue, he seems to concede that it is important to use this criterion, but he is not clear whether the facts show that our government has indeed turned to invasion of Iraq as a last resort.

George A. Lopez

Iraq and Just-War Thinking (p. 136)

George A. Lopez offers us a short review of just-war thinking by our government in several post–World War II military adventures and concludes that it has had little influence — not because alternative moral principles have been relied on but because realpolitik thinking has thrust all moral principles to the side. Lopez (like G. E. M. Anscombe, Peter Steinfels, and Andrew Sullivan) is a Catholic for whom the just-war tradition has special significance, and it is clear that he would like to see the criteria of that tradition playing a larger role in our government's thinking.

Lopez draws the standard distinction between the justice of going to war (*jus ad bellum*) and the justice of the way the war is fought (*jus in bello*), and he dwells on the way in which the latest weaponry — PGMs (precision-guided munitions (para. 8) — causes greater collateral damage (for which read death and injury to noncombatants) than the older weaponry. Worse than that, he points out how the "targets of military necessity" (para. 9) have increased in number and variety, thanks to these "smart weapons." Lopez has no difficulty in criticizing our government for its violation of the principles of *jus in bello*.

He ends his essay on a somewhat forlorn note, regretting the neglect by Catholic moral theologians of just-war thinking (para. 12). He says, in effect, that if Catholic thinkers will not lead the way in this regard, the government and non-Catholics generally cannot be altogether faulted for failing to do better.

William A. Galston

The Perils of Preemptive War (p. 141)

William A. Galston's essay, published on September 23, 2002, during the preliminaries to the U.S.-led invasion of Iraq in March 2003, reviews the arguments of our government in favor of its preemptive attack on Iraq, and he finds those arguments unpersuasive. His critique is, in our judgment, one of the best — perhaps the best — to explain why the invasion was unjustified by any of the relevant criteria, whether prudential or principled. His concluding paragraph lays down the policies that he thinks our government must support if it decides (as it did) to go ahead with the invasion. It is instructive to compare the proposals he makes in this paragraph with what our policy in Iraq actually was in 2003 and will be beyond.

Galston was something of a house philosopher during the first Clinton administration, so he writes about public policy with a certain ease and authority that is uncharacteristic of those with merely academic credentials. This essay we reprint here (written six months before the U.S. invasion of Iraq) discusses the topic of preventive war — a topic ignored in foreign-policy debates provoked by any of our earlier military ventures, from the Spanish American War to the Gulf War. It was brought to the forefront of discussion by the Bush administration as part of its rationale for the invasion of Iraq in 2003.

Galston opens with two quotations, one from the President and the other from the Vice President, both from the summer of 2002, in which the idea of preventive war by our military is advocated by these officials as a legitimate response to the dangerous and lawless behavior of Saddam Hussein, not to mention other tyrants and terrorists.

Preventive war is not to be confused with a war of self-defense. A person (or nation) acts in self-defense when it responds to the aggressive actions of another person (nation). Acting in self-defense using the instruments of war is rarely unjustified, but cannot be a response merely to the likelihood or the possibility of aggression. War undertaken on the grounds of likely or possible aggression is preventive warfare, not self-defense. This is not to say that preventive warfare is always unjustified and that war in self-defense is always justified. Would Nazi Germany have legitimately invoked self-defense if France and Great Britain had decided in 1939 that Germany's behavior toward its neighbors and to Jews warranted armed invasion and preemptive war? Only those with clean hands can invoke self-defense to justify their use of force.

Galston quotes the philosopher Michael Walzer on the proposition that "First strikes can occasionally be justified before the moment of immediate attack, if we have reached the point of 'sufficient threat.' . . ." This concept involves "a manifest intent to injure, a degree of active preparation that makes that intent a positive danger, and a general situation in which waiting or doing anything other than fighting, greatly magnifies the risk" (para. 18). Given that concept, what do the facts about confronting Iraq suggest about the justifiability of our first strike? You might divide the class into two or three groups of three students each and have them look up (with help from the reference librarian) what the print media reported that our government said about these issues in late 2002 and early 2003. The rest of the class could also be divided into groups of three students, their task being to see what critics and interpreters of our government's behavior had to say about these same issues.

Galston's views on this matter are not hard to find, although not every reader of his essay will agree: "the case has not been made that Iraq poses a sufficient threat to justify preemptive action" (para. 21).

Galston is no pacifist, as is clear from his closing paragraphs (16–27), in which he tells the reader how a preemptive war ought to be fought and what kind of peace we must prepare for. Writing these words at the end of the summer of 2003, we are not sure that Galston's recommendations are being or will be followed by our government — and it is certain that at least one of them ("explore and exhaust all other *reasonable* options") has not been satisfied. At the present moment it appears we are clearly at risk of "the destruction and abandonment of a nation," which Galston regards as "absolutely the worse [*sic*] outcome imaginable" (para. 26).

Andrew Sullivan

Yes, a War Would Be Moral (p. 148)

If there is, or was, a case to be made for our invasion of Iraq in 2003, its main features are found in the essay we reprint by Andrew Sullivan. War, according to Sullivan, is not only "sometimes a moral option. . . . Sometimes it is the only moral option" (para. 2). And war against Iraq now is one of those times. Sullivan makes points that many observers overlook or would dispute — namely, that "we are not the aggressor" and that such a war would not be "a new one" (para. 2). Sullivan wants us to look at the invasion of Iraq as a response to Saddam Hussein's unprovoked and uninvited invasion in Kuwait in 1990. After reviewing Saddam's long record of noncompliance with United Nations sanctions, for all practical purposes exhausting peaceful tactics, what else is there for us to do except invade and reduce the likelihood of, if not guarantee against, our becoming the victims of Saddam's weapons of mass destruction?

Sullivan is a Roman Catholic, and he mentions just-war theory, but only in passing (para. 4). He does not attempt to show that the situation in Iraq as of preinvasion 2003 fits four-square with the criteria of *jus ad bellum*. A useful student exercise would be to take G. E. M.

Anscombe's criteria for just war (p. 671) and see the extent to which the facts as Sullivan presents them yield a rationale for invasion.

One noticeable feature of Sullivan's essay is just how uncompromising he is. In his closing paragraph he insists that war against Iraq "is not only vital for our national security; it is "a moral imperative" (para. 6). On the other hand, he notes two contingencies that could nullify this imperative: too many avoidable and unavoidable civilian casualties and an inability or unwillingness to stay the course and turn Iraq into a model democracy. We shall see in the fullness of time whether these contingencies are satisfied.

9
Privacy: What Are Its Limits? (p. 151)

Amitai Etzioni

Less Privacy Is Good for Us (and You) (p. 151)

Although this essay is graceless, we think it makes a good introduction to the topic, partly because it is short, partly because it does not go into subtleties, and partly because it lucidly sets forth a basic issue: How do we balance a right to privacy against considerations of the public interest? We say the essay is graceless. We have in mind such things as the use of *media* as a singular noun (para. 2) (common of course, but still not widely accepted) and the use of *rather* to modify "justifiable diminution of privacy" (para. 3) (the diminution may be justifiable in some instances and not others, but that is different from saying something is "rather justifiable"). He tells us that biometrics will lead to "substantial" benefits (para. 9), a word that seems grotesquely cautious when in the next paragraph he speaks of recovering billions of dollars from criminals, persons who falsify their income taxes, and divorced parents who change their identity to escape their financial obligations to their children.

But, again, in our view these infelicities do not prevent the essay from being a useful way of getting into an important aspect of the topic. Readers will differ in their evaluation of Amitai Etzioni's position, but it is our guess that most students will accept his concluding formulation: Privacy is "one very important right, but not one that trumps most other considerations, especially of public safety and health."

Etzioni says in his next-to-last paragraph that "Privacy should rely squarely on the Fourth Amendment." This amendment distinguishes between searches that are "unreasonable" (and therefore violate privacy) and searches that are acceptable because they are supported by evidence of "probable cause." In Etzioni's view, the latter searches are "those that enhance the common good to such an extent that they are justified, even if they intrude into one's privacy." We quote the amendment:

> The right of the people to be secure in their persons, houses, papers, and effects, against unreasonable searches and seizures, shall not be violated, and no warrants shall issue but upon probable cause, supported by oath or affirmation, and particularly describing the place to be searched, and the persons or thing to be seized.

Nadine Strossen

Everyone Is Watching You (p. 155)

The title is catchy, but of course it is obviously not true. Nadine Strossen defends the aptness of her title (para. 3), but her list of privacy invaders ("banks, . . . workplaces") falls well short of "everyone." Her entire worry seems to focus on surveillance cameras. But not every street has such cameras recording whoever strolls down the sidewalk. We do not wish to quibble over her use of the inclusive pronoun; we grant that her list of invaders is broad enough to alert us to their lurking in many corners of everyday life, enough to properly alarm us.

We also hesitate to agree with her that our current lifestyles find us "increasingly . . . forfeiting [our] privacy" (para. 3). Normally, one "forfeits" something as a penalty or punishment for wrongdoing. But no such wrongdoing is involved in this context; what is involved is a *loss* of privacy.

Strossen considers and rejects the argument that "we need to trade privacy for safety" (para. 8). We find the anecdotal evidence she cites (paras. 9–11) convincing, as far as it goes. What, however, about the principle itself? Strossen neither endorses nor rejects it. We think it is certainly reasonable to trade a certain amount of privacy for safety. Think, for example, of the x-ray screening of our baggage we all experience as we queue up to board the plane. We have no idea how many mad bombers, angry jilted lovers, drunks, or others who arrive at the gate with a loaded gun are prevented from boarding, thanks to the x-ray surveillance. But we are reassured by the practice every time we have to ride a plane. Reasonable people, of course, can disagree over *how much* privacy to sacrifice to secure a given increment in safety. But the principle itself seems to us unassailable. We wish Strossen had explicitly conceded that point. (Could she claim she had done so, implicitly?)

Strossen is a law professor and president of the American Civil Liberties Union and thus sees herself (rightly) to be a staunch defender of personal privacy; she is skeptical, if not downright hostile, regarding laws that infringe on that privacy. Naturally, she endorses the rulings of the California Supreme Court striking down "methods of surveillance" that invade our privacy with little or no gain in public safety (paras. 12–13). She is less enthusiastic about the current majority on the U.S. Supreme Court and encourages us to "take political or other direct action" to remedy the Court's inaction (para. 15).

What measures does she recommend? (1) Join with others to protest cameras in public places (does that mean cameras are acceptable in bank lobbies or airport terminals?). (2) If you see one in a public place, "find out why it is there" (arrive at the airport or bank an hour or so early, so you can ask some questions?). (3) Refuse to shop at businesses that photorecord all transactions (a tall order today). (4) Tell a prospective employer that "you object to secret taping" (how about taping that is obvious because the camera is visible?). (5) Urge elected officials to enact laws "limiting surveillance" ("limiting" it in what ways and by what methods?). We grant that an alarmed and concerned citizenry is our safest protection against excessive public and private invasions of our privacy. But we suspect that most of us will quietly acquiesce in these current invasions without much if any protest.

Judith Wagner DeCew

The Feminist Critique of Privacy (p. 161)

By the way, the author's name is pronounced as though it were spelled "Dekew."

This is one of the more challenging essays in our book; most readers are unlikely to fully grasp it on a first reading. The reason is twofold. First, the targets of Judith Wagner DeCew's analysis are views on privacy from law professor Catharine MacKinnon, whose prose demands patience and care. Second, the reader has to watch DeCew struggle again and again to make MacKinnon's views sufficiently clear so that they can be fairly and effectively criticized. That, too, requires the reader's patience and care. So let us start out modestly.

In answer to question 1 (and see also DeCew's para. 2), the Fourth Amendment in the federal Bill of Rights protects us "against unreasonable searches and seizures" — that is, against unwarranted invasions of our private property (things that can be "searched" or "seized"). A tort is any harmful wrong to a person (other than a breach of contract or a crime) for which a court will provide a remedy — that is, an invasion of personal safety or privacy where harm is inflicted, typically unintentionally but negligently.

How might a feminist critique of privacy undermine or trivialize the protections that a right of privacy provides or ought to provide? That is the great topic of this essay. The answer comes initially in the paragraph in which DeCew first quotes MacKinnon — a paragraph that she paraphrases and interprets and makes much more accessible. Perhaps the best epigrammatic expression of MacKinnon's position comes at the beginning of DeCew's fifth paragraph, when MacKinnon is quoted as stating that "The private is public for those for whom the personal is political." Some class discussion could usefully be devoted to unpacking this sentence. Readers should find DeCew's interpretation of this phrase and the two claims it contains helpful (para. 5 following the MacKinnon quotation).

Perhaps the best restatement of MacKinnon's position by DeCew (para. 6) leads DeCew to open the next paragraph by stating flatly that MacKinnon's argument — now that we can at last see what it comes to — "is easily refuted." Perhaps. But it takes DeCew the next couple of paragraphs to explain that refutation.

DeCew insists that although MacKinnon blurs the point, "privacy and autonomy are distinct concepts" (para. 7) (question 2), and we fully agree.

We encounter the so-called public/private split first at the end of MacKinnon's remarks in the middle of paragraph 5 and again when DeCew undertakes to "reconstruct" it (para. 8) (question 4). We sympathize with her when she says that, important though his "split" is, "it is difficult to clarify what the feminist critique of it entails." DeCew thinks MacKinnon thinks "there is no distinction between public and private because there is no private realm for women at all" (para. 8). DeCew is reluctant to follow MacKinnon here (and so are we) because a mare's nest of questions arises once you take seriously the idea that there is not and cannot be any private realm for women at all (para. 9). Further light is shed on this point by DeCew's review of the relevant ideas of Jean Bethke Elshtain (para. 9) and Ruth Gavison (para. 10).

Is it really true, as MacKinnon claims (in DeCew's interpretation), that "women have no privacy" (para. 5)? Or is this just exaggeration to catch our attention in a way that a more accurate statement ("many women have little privacy in matters of great importance to them, and some women have none") fails to do? What, after all, is the legitimate role for rhetorical exaggeration in a serious argument? Consider another of her remarks in this vein: "The right of privacy is a right of men 'to be let alone'" (para. 11). The phrase "to be let alone" comes from the famous law review article by Brandeis and Warren. It is difficult, indeed impossible, for us to see the Brandeis-Warren defense of privacy in that article as a protective device for "men 'to be let alone.'" Another epigrammatic exaggeration from MacKinnon? Or a deep penetration below the surface of the concept of privacy? We leave it for the reader to judge.

10
Sexual Harassment:
Is There Any Doubt about What It Is? (p. 174)

Of the four pieces that we reprint, none will cause students any difficulty. We begin the unit with the Tufts University statement, and then continue with Ellen Goodman, who in a very readable middle-of-the-road piece argues that of course there is such a thing as sexual harassment and it is fairly widespread and fairly easily identifiable.

At some point in the discussion you may want to tell students what the Equal Employment Opportunity Commission (EEOC) says about the issue. Here are its "Guidelines on Sexual Harassment," from Title VII, Part 1604.11:

> Harassment on the basis of sex is a violation of Sec. 703 of Title VII. Unwelcome sexual advances, requests for sexual favors, and other verbal or physical conduct of a sexual nature constitute sexual harassment when (1) submission to such conduct is made either explicitly or implicitly a term or condition of an individual's employment, (2) submission to or rejection of such conduct by an individual is used as the basis for employment decisions affecting such individual, or (3) such conduct has the purpose or effect of unreasonably interfering with an individual's work performance or creating an intimidating, hostile, or offensive working environment.

This passage has been fairly widely copied and adapted in codes issued by universities. Here, for instance, is a passage from the University of Minnesota's "Policy Statement on Sexual Harassment." We have italicized the additions.

> For the purposes of this policy, sexual harassment is defined as follows: Unwelcome sexual advances, requests for sexual favors, and other verbal or physical conduct of a sexual nature constitute sexual harassment when (1) submission to such conduct is made either explicitly or implicitly a term or condition of an individual's employment *or academic advancement*, (2) submission to or rejection of such conduct by an individual is used as the basis for employment decisions *or academic decisions* affecting such individual, or (3) such conduct has the purpose or effect of unreasonably interfering with an individual's work performance *or academic performance* or creating an intimidating, hostile, or offensive working *or academic environment*.

Tufts University

What Is Sexual Harassment? (p. 174)

The policy statement, as it stands, is not an argument and does not include any argument. The statement also does not define *sexual harassment*. However, both an implicit definition and an implicit argument can be detected; here's one way of formulating each, beginning in premise (1) with the definition:

1. Sexual harassment consists of unwanted, unwelcome sexual attention by one person from another.
2. Such attention can create an intimidating, hostile social environment for the victim.
3. Whoever creates such an environment ought to be disciplined and, if appropriate, punished.
4. Therefore, whoever sexually harasses another ought to be disciplined and, if appropriate, punished.

The argument as it stands is valid; whether it is sound (that is, proves its conclusion) depends mostly on whether premise (3) is acceptable. We think it is, and so do most opponents of sexual harassment.

In principle, of course, sexual harassment can occur between men and between women, but the predominant mode is heterosexual harassment, with the male party the harasser and the female the one who is harassed.

There is, to be sure, some vagueness in the definition of sexual harassment. Perhaps the most important question is this: Does an unsolicited sexual advance (for example, a hug or a kiss) by a man constitute sexual harassment of a woman if she doesn't want it? Or does it count as harassment only if she also says she doesn't want it, and he refuses to take no for an answer and *persists* anyway? The Tufts policy (perhaps all too typically) does not make it clear whether the former as well as the latter qualifies as sexual harassment. Some feminists are in controversy with the law on this point. Gloria Steinem, founder of the National Women's Political Caucus and of *Ms.* magazine, for example, recently made it clear that for her, there is no sexual harassment until the woman has said "No" to the advancing male (*New York Times*, March 22, 1998). That provoked a critic to point out that the EEOC has ruled that a "No" first was not necessary provided the unwanted conduct was "unusually severe" (*New York Times*, March 28, 1998). Taking sexual harassment seriously was not encouraged when a first-grader in North Carolina was suspended from school for kissing a classmate on the cheek (*New York Times*, March 22, 1998).

Sexual harassment of women by men in the workplace, as a special category of sex discrimination, was outlawed under Title VII of the Civil Rights Act of 1964; the Supreme Court upheld that interpretation in 1968 in *Meritor Savings Bank v. Vinson.* (To this day no federal statute defines *sexual harassment* and makes it unlawful.) With the confirmation hearings in the Senate for Supreme Court nominee Clarence Thomas in 1991, sexual harassment (charged against him by his former assistant, Anita Hill) suddenly went to the head of the national agenda, where it remains today, having been enormously stimulated during the second Clinton administration when charges of sexual harassment were filed against the president by Paula Jones. Under the law, an unwanted sexual overture will not normally count as sexual harassment unless some adverse effect on the unwilling recipient can be shown, for example, denial of a promotion by the employer because the employee refused to submit to the overture. In April 1998 Paula Jones's suit against the president was dismissed by the trial judge in part because she could show no adverse effects on her career from her refusal to submit to the alleged harassment. During 1997, more than 17,000 lawsuits charging sexual harassment were filed with the EEOC (*New York Times,* March 19, 1998).

Colleges and universities are, of course, free to develop their own codes of sexual harassment. The Tufts policy deviates from the prevailing law by not requiring the complainant to show she suffered adverse effects from rejecting unwanted attentions (see the "or" at the end of item (1) in para. (2)).

A good exercise, either in class or as a take-home assignment, would be to try to revise the Tufts policy so that its conception of sexual harassment and the ensuing disciplinary procedures more nearly conform to what the student thinks appropriate — assuming, of course, that there are ways to improve the Tufts policy.

Ellen Goodman

The Reasonable Woman Standard (p. 179)

Our first question following the essay invites students to talk about Ellen Goodman's style. We think part of a classroom session might well be devoted to stylistic matters, though of course stylistic matters (at least in our view) are in the final analysis matters of content. Consider, for example, the end of paragraph 4:

> One boss asks his secretary if he can still say "good morning," or is that sexual harassment. Heh, heh. The women aren't laughing.

What, one might ask the class, is that "heh, heh" doing here? Whether Goodman is imitating the boss, who laughs at his own little joke, or whether she is mockingly speaking in her own person, pretending to laugh at the idiotic joke and thus making clear that the joke is idiotic, the point is evident: It is not amusing when men make jokes about the sexual harassment of women. Men may pretend to be kidding, or they may even believe that they are kidding, but the jokes reveal either an unwillingness to recognize a serious problem, or, more often, they reveal a continued attempt to put women down. That is, the jokes are a way of ridiculing women, who are rightly concerned about a serious problem. Our laborious comment on Goodman's sentences shows, by way of contrast, how effective her colloquial language is. A less colloquial style probably could not have made this point so pointedly.

Although the essay is loosely organized, the thesis is clear enough: Men should try to imagine (and they *can* do this) how a reasonable woman would feel. This may sound a bit murky, but, as Goodman says, "When everything was clear, it was clearly biased. The old single standard was a male standard" (para. 8). She goes on (after a passage in which she ironically asks, "What's a poor man to do?"), to indicate that in fact males *can* empathize sufficiently, just as jurors do when they must put themselves into the role of a reasonable innkeeper or a reasonable train operator — or, for that matter, a reasonable man.

Ellen Frankel Paul

Bared Buttocks and Federal Cases (p. 182)

Professor Ellen Frankel Paul opens her essay with a strongly worded indictment against American men for their sexual harassment of women "in alarming proportions." She then turns (paras. 1–5) to some examples of such harassment. So far, however, we have no definition of this key concept in the discussion; we are left to define the term on the wing, as it were, from the examples she gives (question 3). Eventually she rightly notes (para. 9) that the term "is notoriously ill-defined" — all the more reason for her to help out the reader sooner rather than later. The first indications of how she might define it do not come until her comments on the United Methodist position on the issue (para. 9).

The effect of her silence, intentional or not, is to make it virtually impossible to know what to make of one statistic she cites (para. 8). When she reports that "nearly 80 percent of the respondents reported that they or someone they knew had been victims of sexual harassment," what did these respondents (or those who polled their views) think was the sexual harassment these women had experienced? Would we agree? Without any definition we are at a loss to respond reasonably to this information.

Here's a test: Would Paul accept the definition of the term used in the Tufts statement on the subject (p. 174)? Your students might well be asked to write a 250-word paper in which they compare one of those policy statements with their own proposed definition of sexual harassment as it figures in Paul's essay.

In passing we note a rather odd remark from Paul. She observes, "For women to expect reverential treatment in the workplace is utopian" (para. 6). Normally things described as "utopian" are things we'd love to have, but realistically won't be lucky enough to obtain. Does Paul really want us to think that it would be a marvelous idea, just too good to be true, if women were given "reverential treatment in the workplace"? We think the idea is, well, silly and not utopian at all, and an example of the very hyperbole she condemns two paragraphs later. With apologies to Coventry Patmore (author of "The Angel in the House"), Paul seems to be recommending the angel in the workplace, and we find that as objectionable as the angel in the house.

We heartily endorse the cautions Paul urges on readers in paragraph 10, especially when she says "a sense of proportion needs to be restored" to the discussion (and accusations) of sexual harassment. She singles out the exaggerations of Catharine MacKinnon as representative of the failure to make appropriate distinctions. Paul herself relies on the distinction between the "objectively injurious" and the "subjectively offensive" (para. 14) and between "serious harm" and the "morally offensive" (para. 15). Harmful sexual harassment, she argues, deserves to be treated as a crime or a tort. Offensive harassment she dismisses as unworthy of attention by the courts. She urges women to raise their threshold of the "outrageous" (para. 16) by enduring discomfort "in silence," complaining "to higher management," or getting a different job. "Women," she says, "need to develop a thick skin in order to survive and prosper in the workforce."

We expect many feminists will bridle at these suggestions. But before they do, shouldn't they consider whether the alternatives aren't really worse? What is to be done with "offensive male bores" (her closing phrase) whose bad judgment, lack of self-discipline, and failures of sympathy and imagination make women uncomfortable? Their "trivial offenses, dirty jokes, sexual overtures, and sexual innuendoes" (para. 17) can cause intense discomfort. Is the solution to go to court seeking an injunction, demanding compensation, or threatening prosecution? If legal resources such as these are inappropriate overkill, what is left but confrontation, persuasion, mockery, and anger at those who mistreat women in these offensive but not harmful ways?

Sarah J. McCarthy

Cultural Fascism (p. 189)

Sarah J. McCarthy's argument appeared in *Forbes*, a business-oriented magazine, so it is not surprising that it takes the line it does. It is pretty hard-hitting, beginning with the title, "Cultural Fascism," a theme that is picked up in paragraph 3, where McCarthy speaks of her opponents as "the feminist political correctness gestapo" — that is, as comparable to the hated Nazi secret service police.

To return to the beginning of the essay: The first paragraph uses an ad hominem argument, calling attention to the fact that the call for "lottery-size punitive damages" for sexual harassment (McCarthy *does* have a gift for metaphor!) comes from Senator Ted Kennedy, widely regarded as a womanizer and as the man responsible for the death of a woman who worked for him. The point here is, in effect, "Look who is setting himself up as the defender of women." Still, we find the paragraph powerful, especially since it ends by calling attention to the fact that the senators have voted to exempt themselves from punitive damages. There may be good reasons for their vote, but (at least as McCarthy presents the matter) they do seem like a bunch of rogues.

In the second half of the essay McCarthy several times asserts that she was a feminist activist. She does not, in our view, convincingly support this assertion: She just talks about the good old days when there were "powerful woman writers" (para. 7) and contrasts them with today, an age of "lawyers — prim women and men who went to the politically correct law schools" (para. 8). These New Age feminists, in her view, regard women as "china dolls" and therefore do a disservice to women who, she knows from her experience in the restaurant business, can take the rough stuff that men dish out.

Additional Topics for Critical Thinking and Writing

1. In the text, in question 5, we ask students to provide what McCarthy might offer as a definition of sexual harassment. You may want to vary the assignment by calling attention to the fact that the American Civil Liberties Union has argued that sexual harassment should be defined as expression that (1) is directed at a specific employee — rather than, for instance, a pin-up calendar visible to all passersby — and that (2) "demonstrably hinders or completely prevents his or her continuing to function as an employee." Do you agree with this position, or do you think it is too restricted? Explain.

2. Do you think that only someone who has suffered economic harm — for instance, someone who has been denied raises or who has been fired — should be able to allege that a supervisor has created a "hostile environment"? (This position would mean that a supervisor who repeatedly asked for a date or who made suggestive comments but who did not damage the employee financially would not be said to have created a hostile environment.)

11
Torture: Is It Ever Justifiable? (p. 192)

Torture was first influentially attacked as a desirable method of interrogation by the young Italian jurist Cesare Beccaria (1738–1794) in his influential polemic, *On Crimes and Punishments* (1764) — the short treatise in which he was one of the first secular European thinkers to attack capital punishment. A decade or so later the English philosopher Jeremy Bentham wrote what is probably the earliest serious defense of torture, but it had no influence as it remained unpublished until 1973.

The practice of torture in our society is not unknown. One of the earliest American cases is that of Giles Corey, who was pressed to death in 1692 during the Salem witchcraft trials for his refusal to name names. (The story is dramatized in Arthur Miller's play, *The Crucible*.) So-called third-degree methods have long been used by police to extract confessions and other information not divulged voluntarily, despite the expressed public disapproval of such methods. Techniques of this sort became standard practice by the totalitarian governments in Germany and Russia early in the past century. Torture has a long history and probably a greater future than even many of its advocates would desire.

So much for a few preliminary observations. Selecting from a vast literature, we have reprinted five essays on the topic, four of them quite recent. At one extreme is Dr. Vincent Iacopino, who opposes torture in every form and for any reason. He writes from the perspective of one who has seen the face of torture in its victims, and so his voice has a certain authority that is lacking in the largely academic arguments in the other four essays. Paired with his essay is the defense of torture by Clinton R. Van Zandt, who describes himself as a "security consultant." Van Zandt seems to have but one arrow in his quiver: We need to have recourse to torture because it is the only way to deal with a "ticking bomb" scenario. Iacopino thinks the "ticking bomb" scenario is "naive" and "abstract." Both these writers cannot be correct.

The Iacopino and Van Zandt debate is followed by another debate, this time between two distinguished Harvard Law School professors, Philip B. Heymann and Alan M. Dershowitz. Heymann agrees with Iacopino in wanting to bar torture no matter what the consequences and circumstances; Dershowitz agrees with Van Zandt and Michael Levin, the closing essay in this casebook, all three of whom defend torture as appropriate in special cases. It is useful to study closely the details of these three essays, especially regarding the safety measures each proposes to reduce the likelihood of error and abuse. There are, of course, some notable overlaps among the three defending the use of torture, as one would expect.

Our view, should you be interested, is that Heymann's challenging predictions about what would be the likely consequences of opening the door to torture —however carefully monitored — have not been adequately addressed and answered by those who disagreed with him. His skepticism about the reliability, not to say infallibility, of the officials (judges, prosecutors, police) who would manage the system of torture cannot be dismissed out of hand. Thanks to his service during the Clinton administration in the Department of Justice, his worries are not merely academic. They present sobering considerations, all of which must be dealt with before we can give a green light to torture.

Clinton R. Van Zandt

It Should Be Permissible to Torture Suspected Terrorists to Gather Information (p. 192)

Clinton R. Van Zandt contributes two important considerations in the current debate over the morality and effectiveness of torturing terrorist suspects. The first is his implied suggestion that the "coercive techniques known as 'stress and duress'" (para. 3) are the sort of thing he (and others?) have in mind when they endorse torture today. (But note that before he is done, Van Zandt would empower the government "to do whatever was necessary to obtain the needed information" (para. 5). The second is his proposal for a special national tribunal "before which the government could argue that torture was essential to extract critical information." Van Zandt rather overstates the matter; advocates of torture do not limit themselves to the (rare?) cases where they *know* that the suspect has information they want. No, they condone using torture where the authorities *believe* the suspect has such information — and it is precisely because one's beliefs in this matter can be wrong that the problem of false positives is so troublesome (see the essay by Philip B. Heymann, text p. 195).

Van Zandt does not discuss the issue of false positives; perhaps he can be excused for the omission because his essay is so short (barely 400 words) and he cannot discuss everything. He does find space to mention the favorite stalking horse of torture's advocates, the ticking bomb (para. 6). In his counterpart essay, Vincent Iacopino derides this hypothetical as an "abstract fantasy." We hope he is right.

Vincent Iacopino

It Should Not Be Permissible to Torture Suspected Terrorists to Gather Information (p. 194)

Vincent Iacopino's short essay (about 500 words) — just the sort of length we occasionally suggest for a student essay — takes a categorical position in opposition to torture under any conditions and for any reason (para. 1). Students might be asked to write a short 250-word essay comparing the reasons that Philip B. Heymann (p. 761) gives in opposition to torture with the reasons that Iacopino gives. One might hazard the guess that Heymann the lawyer does a somewhat more skillful job in arguing for his case than does Iacopino the medical researcher.

Iacopino, in his second bullet in para. 2, observes that "Torture does not make any one person or society safe or more secure." Of course, this is true. But information that in theory might be gleaned from an informant who will talk only after torture could make persons and society "safer or more secure." The possibility can't be ruled out a priori.

Philip B. Heymann

Torture Should Not Be Authorized (p. 195)

Alan M. Dershowitz

Yes, It Should Be "On the Books" (p. 198)

One does not see every day a pair of Harvard law professors, such as Alan M. Dershowitz and Philip B. Heymann, slugging it out in public over some issue of policy. Each of these writers develops his argument with enviable skill. It would not surprise us if most readers finish the two essays with their confidence shaken in whichever position they eventually adopt.

The area of disagreement between Dershowitz and Heymann is fairly narrow and precise. Both agree in the moral judgment that torture is undesirable. Both agree in the empirical generalization that the use of torture cannot be entirely eliminated. Their disagreement is over whether the police and other officials should have access to the methods of torture, what conditions (if any) justify its use, and especially whether the use of such methods should be on the books — that is, argued openly before a judge and kept as a matter of public record (para. 5). Dershowitz argues for the affirmative; Heymann, for the negative.

No matter what sort of torture you might think of, it seems safe to say that Heymann is against it. Dershowitz does not tell us what sorts of torture he thinks are appropriate to use under certain circumstances. Here is one extreme possibility: Any form of torture is justified, other things being equal, provided it is believed to be the least painful or harmful act sufficient to extract from the person tortured the information desired by the officials directing the torture. The problem here is twofold: First, we may not have any very clear idea of just which acts of torture will be ruled out by the criterion. Second, the suspect being tortured may not have the information being sought by the torturer, in which case the cruelty of the torture is to no avail. This is the classic problem of the false positives to which both Heymann and Dershowitz allude: A false positive is any prediction of future behavior (in this case, revealing information under torture) that fails to materialize (the suspect does not have the information he or she is being tortured to reveal).

Michael Levin

The Case for Torture (p. 200)

As Professor Michael Levin knows, torture has not received positive press in recent decades, even though it continues to be widely practiced as an interrogation technique in many parts of the world. As the social philosopher Henry Shue has noted, "No other practice except slavery is so universally and unanimously condemned in law and human convention." To which the authors of Amnesty International's *Report on Torture* (1975) added: "At the same time the practice of torture has reached epidemic proportions."

Identifying torture as a human-rights violation did not rise to the level of international human-rights law until after World War II. The basis for all later international prohibitions is Article 5 of the Universal Declaration of Human Rights (1948), which declares that "No one shall be subjected to torture or to cruel, inhumane or degrading treatment or punishment." The same language appears in Article 7 of the International Covenant on Civil and Political Rights (1976). Under the authority of the United Nations Convention against Torture and Other Cruel, Inhuman or Degrading Treatment or Punishment (1984) a special U.N. Committee against Torture has been established. How effective these provisions have been in suppressing torture and punishing torturers is another matter.

No doubt the principal current source of popular awareness of and opposition to torture is Amnesty International, whose Campaign for the Abolition of Torture began in 1972 and continues to the present.

Hypothetical cases to the side (questions 1 and 2), we have difficulty accepting the criterion Levin offers (which we quote) to demark the justified from the unjustified use of torture. (In this vein consider our suggested reply to Levin in question 4.) How many innocent lives need to be saved before torture is justified? Levin does not tell us (how could he?). Above all, how do we avoid the all-too-obvious slippery slope: Once we openly allow torture in the kind of cases Levin accepts, how are we to keep others from loosening the criteria to include persons "very probably" guilty? Or applying the criteria on the basis of an imperfect grasp of the relevant facts? Or turning prematurely to torture when other possibly effective interrogation methods might work? To us, Levin seems remarkably complacent about this nest of problems.

On the other hand, we are reluctant to embrace an absolute human right forbidding torture. Candor requires us to admit that we have no better alternative to offer for the kind of hypothetical cases Levin conjures up. The cases have been designed in such a way that it is all but impossible to reject his conclusion. What one can say is that his hypothetical cases bear little relation to the kinds of cases in which we know torturers today and in the past have done their work.

In addition to Amnesty's *Report on Torture* (1975), two other books might be mentioned because of the light they shed on the actual use of torture — a story quite remote from the considerations that inspire Levin's defense. One is Edward Peters', *Torture* (1985), a historical survey of torture from Greek and Roman times to the recent past. The other is *The Breaking of Bodies and Minds* (1985), edited by Eric Stover and Elena O. Nightingale, full of stories of recent vintage that record the terrors of those at the mercy of torturers.

Part Three

CLASSIC ARGUMENTS

Plato

Crito (p. 207)

The headnote in the text gives a fairly full account of the context of Crito, both in Socrates' life and in Plato's dialogues. After decades of relative neglect, this dialogue, with its argument over the citizen's obligation to the state, has recently aroused interest among scholars, and several good books (among them those by A. D. Woozley and Richard Kraut) now are available to guide the interested reader through the intricacies of Plato's text.

The dialogue can be divided into three parts of unequal length and importance. In the brief first part (which ends when Crito says "Your death means a double calamity for me"), Plato does little more than set the stage. In the longer second part (which ends when Socrates offers the plea of "the Laws and Constitution of Athens"), Crito makes his feeble attempt to persuade Socrates to escape, and Socrates in rather leisurely fashion examines and rejects Crito's reasons. The final and longest part is also the most important because in it Socrates advances an early version of the social-contract argument for political obligation, later made famous and influential by Locke and Rousseau and revived in recent years in the sophisticated moral philosophy of John Rawls (see his *A Theory of Justice* [1971]). Socrates makes no attempt to rebut this long argument; the reader (along with Crito) is led to think that Socrates must, in all honesty, concede each step and so draw the conclusion the Laws want him to draw.

As for the adequacy of this argument (question 6), the notion of a "just agreement" between the individual citizen and the abstract state looks quite implausible if taken literally, even in the city-state of Athens. But if taken as a metaphor or as a model of an ideal relationship between the individual and the laws, then one has to answer this question: How can a hypothetical or ideal relation impose any actual or real obligation on anyone? The result is a classic dilemma for social-contract theorists, not easily resolved.

The dialogue can be effectively paired with Martin Luther King Jr.'s "Letter from Birmingham Jail" (p. 293). The most obvious difference between the positions of Socrates and King (questions 8 and 9) is that

Socrates implies that the laws of Athens are just — though, unfortunately, wrongly applied to Socrates himself by his Athenian judges —
whereas King asserts that the laws of Alabama are unjust and implies
their application to him is unjust. In particular, Socrates implies that
he gave his free and informed consent to the authority of Athens's laws,
whereas King implies that black Americans never gave their free consent to segregation laws.

Plato

Myth of the Cave (p. 222)

In our headnote to this selection we give something of the context
in the *Republic* in which Plato embeds his Myth, but you may want to
reread some of that context in the dialogue before teaching this selection. Our excerpt is taken from the Desmond Lee translation (Pen-
guin), but several other good modern translations are now available in
paperback in case the Lee is unavailable. Probably the most widely
used still is the well-known Cornford translation (Oxford). The two
most recent translations are by Grube (Hackett) and by Sterling and
Scott (Norton). Slightly older is the edition by Bloom (Basic); of them
all, this one is an attempt to be the most literal (but no one thinks it
improves on Shorey's in this respect), and it also provides a long (and
controversial) interpretive essay on the whole dialogue. Consulting any
one of these translations for the context of the Myth, or for a different
version of the Myth itself, coiuld prove rewarding.

While we're at it, it's appropriate to think about the word "Myth"
in the present context. The "Myth" of the Cave is also often called an
"allegory" or "simile"; Cornford even calls it a "parable." It is perhaps
obvious enough why it could be so variously described, especially
when choice among these terms is not a matter of finding the best English word for one Greek term. Insofar as Plato himself uses some one
term to refer to this passage, it is *eikon*, "image." Moreover, of them all,
myth may be the most misleading, for it is clear that Socrates is not
mythologizing for Glaucon's benefit, but only telling a vividly detailed
story to make graphic some basic teachings. Paul Friedlander, in volume III of his *Plato* (pp. 134 ff.), does give a brief discussion of the
"mythopoeic" aspects of the whole dialogue — they are indeed there —
but he does so without referring to the Myth of the Cave.

The reader who wants more help in understanding Plato will find
it most conveniently in the recent *Companion to Plato's Republic*, by
Nicholas P. White. Less recent and less technical but more readable is

Plato's Republic: A Philosophical Commentary, by R. C. Cross and A. D. Woozley. In Chapter 6, they give a nice discussion of the so-called sun and line passages in *Republic* that pave the way for the Myth of the Cave. It is to these passages that Socrates refers when he says, "this simile must be connected throughout with what preceded it." For a convenient and complete translation of all Plato's dialogues, the Bolligen edition by Hamilton and Cairns has no rivals.

One of the basic ideas under attack in the Myth is what Socrates calls "the conception of education professed by those who say that they can put into the mind knowledge that was not there before." Elsewhere, for instance in *Meno*, Plato has Socrates defend the ideal that all our knowledge is already "in" our minds and only needs to be brought to conscious awareness; this is the doctrine that Knowledge is Recollection. Taken in its crudest form, it is utterly unconvincing. But taken in the form in which we have it here in the Myth — as Socrates describes it, "our argument indicates that [there is] a capacity which is innate in each man's mind" — the doctrine seems trivial and obvious. Who would contest that the bare capacity to learn is not implanted by the teacher but instead is presupposed by any effort to teach or learn? Obvious or not, the view Socrates defends certainly is true.

The same can be said of his thesis, more important in the context of the Myth that society cannot be best governed either by academics — "those who are allowed to spend all their lives in purely intellectual pursuits" — or by yahoos — "the uneducated." Whether something analogous to the nation's military service academies (West Point comes much closer to what Plato has in mind as the proper educational setting for his "guardians" than most colleges) is the ideal training ground for future political leaders (Plato, of course, would say "rulers") is more controversial. But these details, because they do not appear directly in the Myth itself, may be safely left unresolved.

Thomas More

From Utopia *(p. 231)*

For a sampling of the amazing variety of interpretations of Thomas More's *Utopia*, one has only to look at the essays reprinted in the Norton Critical Edition of *Utopia* (1975), edited by Robert M. Adams. *Utopia* has been seen, for example, as a book advocating Christianity (in particular, Roman Catholicism), communism, or colonialism. It seems fairly clear to us, however, that More is not advocating any of these things, at least not as an end in itself. Rather, in this humanistic work he is giving his version of an ideal state based on *reason* alone. But he is a Christian speaking to Christians; presumably his sixteenth-century readers were supposed to say to themselves, "If people without revelation can achieve this degree of decency, surely we, with Christ's help, can achieve more. Our society is far inferior to Utopia; let us strive to equal and then to surpass it."

Perhaps the best short essay on *Utopia* is Edward Surtz's introduction to the Yale paper edition, though Father Surtz sees the book as more Christian than do many other commentators. Among Surtz's points are these:

1. The Utopians are typically Renaissance people, balancing Epicureanism with Christianity, having the best of both worlds. They pursue personal pleasure "until it conflicts with social or religious duties, that is, with the just claims of God or fellow citizens" (p. xiv). The term "pleasure" covers many kinds of actions, from scratching an itch to doing virtuous deeds.

2. Utopian communism "is not an end in itself but the best means to the end: pleasure for all the citizens collectively as well as individually" (p. xiv). "The ultimate Utopian ideal of communism is . . . to be of one mind. . . . Sharing material possessions can succeed only if there is first one heart and soul in all" (p. xv).

3. Modern critics too often emphasize More's political, social, and economic innovations and neglect his opinions on education, ethics, philosophy, and religion.

4. More's Utopians are not saints; some are even criminals. More does *not* believe, as some moderns do, that people can be conditioned (brainwashed) to think they are freely cooperating in a society that in fact enslaves them. More's Utopians have some leeway, as in the choice of an occupation and in the use of leisure. Believing in the immutability of the soul, they believe that one's final end is not worship of the state but union with the Absolute.

Most students, when asked for the meaning of *Utopian*, will come up with such pejorative words as *unrealistic, impractical, escapist*. They will be surprised, then, to see how realistic More's view of human nature is. He is fully aware, for instance, of such vices as laziness and, especially, pride — not only in non-Utopian countries but even in Utopia. Indeed, he seems to feel that most of our ills are due to pride. To restrain pride, almost all Utopians must engage in manual labor and must wear a simple garment, and, again to restrain pride, there is no private property. Notice that More does not put the blame for our wicked actions entirely on private property or on any other economic

factors. True, he does say that Europeans greedily seek to attain super-
fluities because they fear they may some day be in want, but it is evident that even Utopia has wrongdoers. That is, even the Utopian
system cannot prevent some people from engaging in wicked behavior.
More does think, however, that some systems allow our wicked natures
to thrive, and so he devises a political, economic, and social system
that keeps down pride (the root of the other deadly sins).

But it is not only pride that is kept in check. Utopia is severely regulated in many ways. For instance, Utopians are free to do what they
wish during their leisure time — provided that they don't loaf, gamble,
or hunt. Similarly, they are free to talk — provided that they don't talk
politics, except at special times. Discussion of state affairs, except at
the appointed times and places, is punishable by death. Orwell's Big
Brother is present in More's Utopia, but R. W. Chambers is probably
right when he argues (in his *Thomas More* [1935]) that Utopia is found-
ed not on terrorism but on "religious enthusiasm," in particular on
faith in God and in the immortality of the soul. Still, even "religious
enthusiasm" has, for many readers, something unpleasant about it —
something too monastic, too rigid, too disciplined, too cold.

Although one understands and sympathizes with More's condemnation of the pride that engenders social injustice, one can't help but
feel that Utopia, with its rational distribution of labor and its evening
lectures on edifying topics, is the poorer for lacking the messy vitality of
life. (In Utopia, everything seems terribly static: The constitution doesn't
change, population is fixed, clothing is uniform, freedom of thought is
limited.) On the other hand, we must remember that in the Europe of
More's day (and still in much of the world) the masses had to toil from
sunrise to sunset to live at a subsistence level. Today's college students
(and their professors) find More's Utopia overly restrictive, but they
should remember that (1) it is a society of material prosperity for all citizens and a society with a good deal of leisure and (2) it was freer and
more tolerant than any of the European societies of its day.

Additional Topics for Critical Thinking and Writing

1. Can it be said that whatever the merits or weaknesses of More's
    proposal, he has astutely diagnosed the problems of society?

2. More's spokesman says that European society "is a conspiracy
    of the rich to advance their own interests under the pretext of
    organizing society" (para. 4). Can the same be said of our soci-
    ety? Explain.

3. Is More's view of human nature "utopian" in the modern sense
    of the word — that is, is it uncharacteristically benign? Explain.

Niccolò Machiavelli

From The Prince *(p. 246)*

Harvey Mansfield Jr., in the introduction to his translation of *The Prince* (1985), argues that for Niccolò Machiavelli the only moral laws are those made by human beings: "The rules or laws that exist are those made by governments or other powers acting under necessity, and they must be obeyed out of the same necessity. Whatever is necessary may be called just or reasonable, but justice is no more reasonable than what a person's prudence tells him he must acquire for himself, or submit to, because men cannot afford justice in any sense that transcends their own preservation" (p. xi).

This reading seems, in a way, much like Marx, who argues that ideology (including ideas of justice) is created by the ruling class, though Marx also seems to believe that because this class achieved power through historical necessity, its ideals — during the period in which it holds power — indeed are true. Witness Marx's praise of the bourgeoisie for redeeming the masses from the "idiocies" of rural life.

Perhaps the heart of the issue is this: Although we may believe that we should be governed by people of honor, Machiavelli (and most utilitarians) would argue that personal goodness and political usefulness are distinct things. A person may be an adulterer, a liar, a sadist, or whatever but may still be an effective guardian of the state. Or, expressed more mildly, a governor may sometimes have to sacrifice personal morality for the safety of the state. Bernard Williams argues, in *Public and Private Morality* (Stuart Hampshire, ed. [1978]), that to preserve civilized life, we need politicians who can bring themselves to behave more badly than we ourselves could do. We want them to be as good as possible — and certainly not to be people who act wickedly on a whim or take pleasure in acting wickedly — but to be able to sacrifice personal moral values for political ones. (This idea makes for lively class discussion.)

A related point: If a leader is widely regarded as immoral, he or she loses an important strength, the goodwill of the public. A small example: A senator who is known to have extramarital affairs can probably survive and can be an effective and even an important senator, but a senator who is regarded as a lecher probably cannot.

On the question of whether cruelty may be beneficial to the state: Machiavelli apparently believed that before a state can be justly ruled, there must be a ruler, and to survive the ruler must be cunning and ruthless. One wonders, of course, if a person with these qualities will also act reasonably, using power for the well-being of the state rather than for purely personal goals. Machiavelli, living in the turmoil of early sixteenth-century Italy, concentrates on the qualities necessary for a leader to survive. Thomas More (see the previous selection in the text), on the other hand, shows us a Utopia with almost no political problems, and thus he can concentrate on the morality of the state rather than on the personal characteristics of the governors. Or put it this way: In Machiavelli, it is the ruler against his rivals and his subjects, whereas in More it is society against the individual's unruly passions.

Additional Topics for Critical Thinking and Writing

1. Imitating Machiavelli's style, notably his use of contrasting historical examples, write an essay of 500 words, presenting an argument on behalf of your own view of some quality necessary in a leader today. You may, for example, want to argue that a leader must be a master of television appearances or must be truthful, compassionate, or versed in history. Your essay will, in a sense, be one chapter in a book called *The Prince Today*.

2. James M. Burns's biography of President Franklin Delano Roosevelt (1882–1945) is titled *Roosevelt: The Lion and the Fox* (1956). Judging from your rereading of Chapter XVIII of *The Prince*, indicate in a paragraph the characteristics of Roosevelt that the biographer is suggesting by this title. Read Burns's biography, and write a 1,000-word essay in which you evaluate the aptness of the title, given the facts about Roosevelt's career and Machiavelli's views.

Jonathan Swift

A Modest Proposal (p. 256)

Our discussion in these notes of Judy Brady's "I Want a Wife" (p. 309) offers a few general comments on satire, some of which are relevant to Jonathan Swift.

Unlike Brady's essay, where the title in conjunction with the author's name immediately alerts the reader that the essay cannot be taken straight, Swift's essay does not provide an obvious clue right away. In fact, some students don't perceive the irony until it is pointed out to them. Such imperceptiveness is entirely understandable. Swift's language is somewhat remote from twenty-first-century language, and in any case students don't expect satire in a collection of arguments. Moreover, it's hard today to know when a projector (the eighteenth-century name for someone with a bright idea) is kidding. A student who has not understood that "A Modest Proposal" is a satire may be extremely embarrassed on learning the truth in public. To avoid this possibility we usually begin the discussion by talking about Swift as a satirist who is known chiefly through *Gulliver's Travels,* and so on.

Most commentators on "A Modest Proposal" have concentrated on the persona of the speaker — his cool use of statistics, his way of regarding human beings as beasts ("a child just dropped from its dam," in para. 4, for example, or his reference to wives as "breeders," in para. 6), and, in short, his unawareness of the monstrosity of his plan to turn the children into "sound, useful members of the commonwealth" (para. 2), a plan that, by destroying children, will supposedly make the proposer "a preserver of the nation" (para. 2). Much of this complacent insensitivity and even craziness is apparent — on rereading — fairly early, as in the odd reference (para. 1) to "three, four, or six children" (what happened to five?), or, for that matter, in the phrases already quoted from paragraph 2. And of course it is true that one object of Swift's attack is the persona, a figure who, despite his profession that he is rational, practical, and compassionate, perhaps can be taken as an emblem of English indifference to Irish humanity. (But the speaker is an Irishman, not an Englishman.) More specifically, the leading object of attack can be said to be political reformers, especially those who heartlessly bring statistics ("I calculate," "I have reckoned," "I have already computed") where humane feelings should rule.

It is less often perceived, however, that the satire is also directed against the Irish themselves, with whom Swift was, by this time, fed up. "Satire" is almost too mild a word for the vehemence of "savage indignation" (Swift's own epitaph refers to his *saeva indignatio*) with which Swift denounces the Irish. Yes, he in effect says, the English treat the Irish abominably, but the Irish take no reasonable steps to help themselves. Even in so small a detail as the proposer's observation that his plan would cause husbands to stop beating pregnant wives (para. 26), we hear criticism not of the English but of the Irish. The chief denunciation of the Irish is evident, however, in the passage beginning with paragraph 29, in which Swift lists the "other expedients" that indeed the Irish themselves could (but do not) undertake to alleviate their plight.

In short, commentators who see Swift's essay simply as a scathing indictment of English hard-heartedness are missing much of the point. One can almost go so far as to say that Swift's satire against the projector is directed not only against his impracticality and his unconscious cruelty but also against his folly in trying to help a nation that, out of stupidity and vanity, obstinately refuses to help itself. The projector sees the Irish as mere flesh; Swift at this time apparently saw them as something more exasperating, flesh that is stupid and vain. Swift was, we think, more than half in earnest when he had his crazy projector say, "I desire the reader will observe, that I calculate my remedy for this one individual kingdom of Ireland and for no other that was, is, or, I think ever can be upon earth."

If you wish students to do some research, you can ask them to look at Swift's "Irish Tracts" (*Prose Works*, ed. Herbert Davis, 12: 1–90, especially *Intelligencer* 19: 54–61), where they will find Swift arguing for the "other expedients" that his projector dismisses.

Related points:

1. This essay has ample material to demonstrate the use of the method that Aristotle calls "the ethical proof"; that is, the pleader's use of his or her ethical character to persuade an audience. (Of course, here it backfires: We soon see a monster, not a benevolist.) Thus, in paragraph 1 the author shows his moral sensibility in using such expressions as "melancholy object" and "helpless infants." Also relevant is the projector's willingness to listen to other views — which he then of course always complacently rejects.

2. A scattering of anti–Roman Catholic material (for example, references to "papists") indicates that the speaker, for all his insistence on his objectivity, is making a prejudiced appeal to emotions.

3. Instructors interested in satiric techniques will probably want to call attention to Swift's abundant use of diminution, such as people reduced to animals and to statistics.

Additional Topics for Critical Thinking and Writing

1. Drawing only on the first three paragraphs, write a brief characterization (probably three or four sentences) of the speaker — that is, of the persona whom Swift invents. Do not talk about Swift the author; talk only about the anonymous speaker of these three paragraphs. Support your assertions by quoting words or phrases from the paragraphs.

2. In an essay of 150 to 250 words, characterize the speaker of "A Modest Proposal," and explain how Swift creates this character. You may want to make use of your answer to the previous question, pointing out that at first we think such-and-such, but later, picking up clues that Swift provides, we begin to think thus-and-so. You may wish, also, to devote a few sentences to the last paragraph of Swift's essay.

3. What is the speaker arguing for? What is Swift arguing for?

4. Write a modest proposal of your own, suggesting a solution to some great social problem. Obvious topics include war, crime, and racism, but choose any topic that almost all people agree is a great evil. Do not choose a relatively controversial topic, such as gay rights, vivisection, gun control, or right-to-work laws. Your proposed solution should be, like Swift's, outrageous, but your essay should not be silly. In the essay you should satirize some identifiable way of thinking.

5. The same basic assignment as the previous one, but this time write an essay on a topic that is controversial and on which you have strong feelings.

Thomas Jefferson

The Declaration of Independence (p. 264)

In discussing almost any argument (for that matter, in discussing any writing) it is usually helpful to consider the intended or imagined *audience(s)*. With minimal assistance students can see that the Declaration of Independence has several audiences (question 1). These audiences can perhaps be described thus:

1. The "candid world" (para. 5), addressed out of "a decent respect to the opinions of mankind" (para. 1);

2. The King and his ministers (the grievances are blamed on them);

3. The British people (students who do a research paper on the Declaration will learn that some passages censuring the British people were deleted to maintain good relations);

4. France (the Declaration announces that the "United Colonies" have "full power to levy War, conclude Peace, contract Alliances, establish Commerce, and to do all other Acts and Things which Independent States may of right do") (most historians see in these words a bid for foreign aid — military supplies from France); and

5. Those colonists who were not eager for independence.

Attention may be given to the *speaker* of the Declaration — that is, to the self-image (question 3) that the colonists present. Jefferson refers to "a decent respect to the opinions of mankind" (para. 1), and he admits that "Governments long established should not be changed for light and transient causes" (para. 4). Notice too his assertion that "We have petitioned for redress in the most humble terms" (para. 33). In short, the colonists present themselves not as radicals or firebrands but as patient, long-suffering people who are willing to put their case before the tribunal of the world. Notice such words as *duty, necessary,* and *necessity.* They are not rebels; rather, they have been "plundered" and "ravaged" and are exerting a right — the right of the people to alter or to abolish a government that fails to fulfill the legitimate purpose of government (para. 4).

Some attention in class can also be profitably given to discussing the *structure* of the work:

1. The first sentence announces the colonists' purpose, explaining "the causes which impel them to the separation."
2. The core of the document is an exposition of the causes, in two sections:
   a. Theoretical and general justification (for example, "self-evident" truths) and
   b. The list of despotic British actions.
3. The Declaration concludes with the response of the colonies (the signers pledge their lives).

Students can also be shown how the explicit assumptions of the Declaration —

1. All men are created equal and are endowed with "unalienable rights."
2. Governments are instituted to preserve these rights.
3. People have a duty and a right to throw off a despotic government.

— can be cast into this *syllogism*:

1. If a government is despotic, the people have a right to overthrow it and to form a new government.
2. The British government of the American colonies is despotic.
3. Therefore, the people have a right to overthrow it and to form a new government.

The major premise is not argued but is asserted as an "unalienable right." The minor premise is arrived at inductively (instances are cited, and a generalization is drawn from them).

Additional Topics for Critical Thinking and Writing

1. The Declaration is an argument for revolution in a particular society. Investigate conditions in some society (for example, Cuba, China, Iran, El Salvador, Nicaragua), and argue that, on the grounds of the Declaration, people in that society do — or

do not — have the right to revolt.

2. Read Chapter 19 of John Locke's *Essay Concerning Civil Government* (first published in 1690), and write a 500-word essay in which you identify all those passages or ideas found in Locke that appear also in the Declaration. Are there any ideas in Locke's chapter that have no parallel in the Declaration, but that nevertheless seem to you to be relevant to its purpose and content?

Elizabeth Cady Stanton

Declaration of Sentiments and Resolutions (p. 269)

Elizabeth Cady Stanton's Declaration of 1848 is the historic precursor of the decade-long effort that finally failed in 1982 to enact an Equal Rights Amendment (ERA) to the Constitution. The Fourteenth Amendment, enacted twenty years after the first Woman's Rights Convention at Seneca Falls, New York, did provide that no state "shall . . . deprive any person of life, liberty, or property without due process of law, nor deny any person within its jurisdiction the equal protection of the laws." At face value, that might look like the rejection of gender as a basis for lawful discrimination. Opponents of the ERA in the 1970s who professed sympathy with feminist claims for constitutional equality often pointed to the language quoted as if that settled the matter. Not so, however.

The term *male* entered the Constitution in the Fourteenth Amendment itself (see section 2), thereby helping to etch more clearly the implicit and historic male bias of the Constitution and the laws from the beginning and indicating that "due process" and "equal protection" were not to be given a gender-free reading. An Illinois case of 1873 settled this issue for decades. Arguing that she was entitled under the Fourteenth Amendment to be admitted to the bar, Myra Bradwell unsuccessfully fought her case through the state courts to the U.S. Supreme Court. The language of the majority's decision enshrined in constitutional interpretation the worst excesses of male chauvinism (see *Bradwell v. Illinois*, 83 U.S. 130 [1873]). Even the right to vote ("elective franchise") (para. 4) was not incorporated into the Constitution until 1920 (the Nineteenth Amendment). Full equality of the sexes under the laws and the Constitution, whether or not it is a good thing, still does not exist in our society.

Civil death (question 3) is the ultimate extreme to which a person can be reduced: denial by law of all civil rights, privileges, immunities, and liberties. (Not even prisoners on death row, today, suffer civil

death.) Stanton elaborates the point (paras. 9–11). It was commonplace among feminists of the previous century to point out that marriage under law was functionally equivalent to civil death.

It was not, however, functionally equivalent to chattel slavery
(which was to last another fifteen years after the Seneca Falls Convention; not surprisingly, the women who organized the convention were
staunch abolitionists). It might be a useful classroom exercise for students to explore the differences under law in the 1840s between the
status of American white women, as the Declaration reports it, and the
status of American black slaves. An excellent source for slave law is A.
Leon Higginbotham Jr., *In the Matter of Color* (1978).

Virginia Woolf

Professions for Women (p. 274)

Woolf's essay is highly personal, although its title might suggest
something highly impersonal. On the surface the essay is narrative
(autobiography) and expository (what it takes to become a writer —
paper, not Paris and masters or mistresses), but like almost all good
writing the essay advances a thesis; that is, it carries an argument. The
thesis, briefly, is that a woman writer must overcome those forces that
keep telling her to write not as a human being but as the sympathetic,
pure, young creature of the bourgeois male's fantasies. This role, which
would require her to conceal her real views of "human relations,
morality, sex," would, Woolf says, have "plucked the heart out of [her]
writing" (para. 3). One must be oneself, and para. 4 argues that not
until women participate "in all the arts and professions" can a woman
know what it is to be herself. (Students may need to be reminded that
when Woolf delivered this talk, in 1931, women were all but barred
from the most prestigious professions, that is, from the clergy, medicine, university teaching, law, and so on.) She lived in a society, she
argues, that did not allow women to speak their minds and that consequently did not allow women to know themselves.

The argument is conducted with great wit (e.g., the joke in para. 1
that "one can buy paper enough to write all the plays of Shakespeare
— if one has a mind that way") and with considerable indirection,
notably in the figure of the Angel in the House, and, more veiled, in the
strongly sexual figure (para. 5) of the fisherwoman whose imagination
is roused from a daydream by "a smash," "an explosion," "something
hard," in short, a thought about "the passions which . . . was unfitting
for her as a woman to say." A moment later, in para. 6, she is more

explicit, when she speaks of "telling the truth about my own experiences as a body."

The final paragraph nicely compliments Woolf's audience by asserting that Woolf's "professional experiences" are also theirs, and nicely complements the first paragraph, in which she also uses the words "professional experiences." This final paragraph is less witty — and more directly outspoken — than the earlier paragraphs, for now she speaks of "fighting . . . formidable obstacles." In the paragraph she continues to praise the audience ("You have won rooms of your own in the house hitherto exclusively owned by men") but cautions that the battle is not yet won ("the room is your own, but it is still bare").

In short, the essay lends itself admirably to a study of tone, especially to the ways in which a writer adjusts to an audience, instructing it without condescending.

George Orwell

Shooting an Elephant (p. 280)

George Orwell explicitly tells us that his experience as a police officer in Burma was "perplexing and upsetting" (para. 2). He characterizes himself as "young and ill-educated" at the time (clearly in the past), and he says he was caught between his hatred of imperialism and his rage against the Burmese. The essay's paradoxical opening sentence foreshadows its chief point (that imperialism destroys the freedom of both the oppressor and the oppressed), but Orwell devotes the rest of the first paragraph, with its ugly characterizations of the Burmese, to dramatizing his rage. Students unaware of Orwell's preoccupation with decency may fail to understand that the first two paragraphs do not contradict but are deliberate; they show the alienation from normal feelings, the violations of self that were, as Orwell goes on to show, the by-products of his role.

That he was playing a role — but a role that captured the player — is highlighted by the theatrical metaphors that accumulate as he is about to shoot the elephant: he sees himself as a "conjurer" with a "magical rifle," as an "actor," and as "an absurd puppet" (para. 7).

The essay's final paragraph, with its cold tone, its conflicting half-truths and rationalizations, again effectively dramatizes the deadening of feeling and loss of integrity Orwell experienced and that he believes all who turn tyrant experience.

Martin Luther King Jr.

I Have a Dream (p. 287)

The setting (the steps of the Lincoln Memorial, in Washington, D.C., on the centennial of the Emancipation Proclamation) plays an important part in this speech. By the way, few students know that the Emancipation Proclamation did not in fact free any slaves. In 1862 President Lincoln announced that he would declare free the slaves of any state that did not return to the Union. None of the states that had seceded accepted the invitation to return, and so on January 1, 1863, he announced the Emancipation Proclamation. It did not apply to slaves in states such as Maryland and Kentucky that had chosen to stay in the Union, and of course it had no force in the Confederacy. Still, the symbolic importance of the Proclamation was and is immense, and it is part of King's speech.

King's association with Lincoln is evident not only in the setting but also in the language. The opening words, "Five Score," evoke the "Four score and seven years ago" of the Gettysburg Address; and Lincoln himself was evoking the language of the Bible. King's speech, too, richly evokes the Bible ("dark and desolate valley," "God's children," "cup of bitterness," "trials and tribulations," "storms of persecution," "every hill and mountain shall be made low, the rough places will be made straight, and the glory of the Lord shall be revealed, and all flesh shall see it together" — this last from Isaiah 40: 4–5).

Another symbol, in addition to Lincoln and to the Bible, is the "American dream" (para. 11, but foreshadowed in the title of the speech), which King, like most other Americans, identifies with the remark in the Declaration of Independence that "All men are created equal." King also identifies his dream (and himself) with "My country, 'tis of thee," and (in the final paragraph) with black spirituals.

The exalted language of the Bible and the Declaration is joined with the humble language of commerce, the "promissory note," the "bad check" of paragraphs 3 and 4, and the whole (because it is a speech) is rich in evocative repetition, especially parallelisms (again a biblical device).

All these devices and allusions are fairly obvious, and that is part of their point. King is emphasizing that speaker and audience share a culture; and though the immediate audience, in Washington, was predominantly black, King knew that his words would also reach a larger audience of whites — whites who share this culture.

The structure (question 6) is this: The first part gives a historical perspective; the second, an exhortation not to fall into evil; the third, an exposition of the dream, a picture of the better world that they can help to bring about.

Additional Topic for Critical Thinking and Writing

King's speech stresses the twin themes of equality and freedom and does not suggest that the two might be in tension or conflict with each other. Do you agree that there is no tension? Try to state precisely the freedom(s) and equalities for which King pleads. Is our society any closer to achieving these goals today, do you think, than in 1963?

Martin Luther King Jr.

Letter from Birmingham Jail (p. 292)

Martin Luther King Jr.'s letter was prompted by a letter by eight Birmingham clergymen. His letter is unusually long ("Never before have I written so long a letter") because he was jailed at the time and thus was unable to speak to audiences face to face.

King here goes to some length to show that his work is thoroughly in the American (and Judeo-Christian) tradition. That is, although he rebuts the letter of the eight clergymen, he represents himself not as a radical or in any way un-American (and of course not as an opponent of the Judeo-Christian tradition), but as one who shares the culture of his audience. Thus, although he rejects the clergymen's view that he is impatient, he begins by acknowledging their decency. They are, he says, "men of genuine goodwill" — and in saying this King thereby implies that he too is a man of goodwill. Moreover, King's real audience is not only the eight clergymen but all readers of his letter, who are assumed to be decent folk. Notice, too, in his insistence that he is speaking on an issue that involves all Americans, his statement that "injustice anywhere is a threat to justice everywhere" (para. 4). But his chief strategy early in the letter is to identify himself with Paul (para. 3) and thus to guide his mainly Christian audience to see him as carrying on a tradition that they cherish. Notice also the references to Niebuhr, Buber (a Jew), and Jesus.

It is usual, and correct, to say that King is a master of the appeal to emotion. This essay reveals such mastery, as when he quotes a five-year-old boy: "Daddy, why do white people treat colored people so mean?" (para. 14). And because King is really addressing not so much the eight clergymen as a sympathetic audience that probably needs encouragement to persist rather than reasons to change their beliefs, an emotional (inspirational) appeal is appropriate. But the essay is also rich in lucid exposition and careful analysis, as in paragraph 6 (on the four steps of a nonviolent campaign) and paragraphs 15 and 16 (comparing just and unjust laws).

Additional Topics for Critical Thinking and Writing

1. Think of some injustice that you know something about, and jot down the facts as objectively as possible. Arrange them so that they form an outline. Then, using these facts as a framework, write an essay (possibly in the form of a letter to a specific audience) of about 500 words, presenting your case in a manner somewhat analogous to King's. For example, don't hesitate to make comparisons with biblical, literary, or recent historical material, to use personal experiences, or to use any other persuasive devices you wish, including appeals to the emotions. Hand in the objective list along with the essay.

2. If some example of nonviolent direct action has recently been in the news, such as actions by persons fearful of nuclear power plants, write an essay evaluating the tactics and their effectiveness in dealing with the issue.

3. Read Plato's *Crito*, and also Plato's *Apology* (in your library). Write an essay of 500 words explaining whether, as King says, "Socrates practiced civil disobedience."

Judy Brady

I Want a Wife (p. 309)

Incidental passages of satire, employing an ironic voice, appear throughout the book, but Judy Brady's essay, like Jonathan Swift's "A Modest Proposal" in Chapter 5, is satiric from beginning to end. Since our book is chiefly about argument (reasoning) rather than about the broader topic of persuasion, we discuss irony very briefly. And because of our emphasis on engaging the audience's goodwill by presenting oneself as benign, we advise students to think twice before they use irony in their arguments. Still, Brady's essay offers an opportunity to talk about the power of verbal irony or satire — in Frank O'Connor's definition, "The intellectual dagger opposing the real dagger."

In talking about this satire, one can point out that in "I Want a Wife," as in much other satire, the persona more or less appears as an innocent eye, a speaker who merely describes, in a simple, objective way, what is going on. (The reader, not the speaker, says, "This is outrageous." The speaker never explicitly states her thesis.) Thus, in the essay Brady is not a creature with a name but merely a member of a class. She is simply "a Wife." We then get the terrifying list of things that a Wife finds thrust on her. These are scarcely described in detail, but the mere enumeration of the chores becomes, by the volume of its unadorned accumulation, comic — and stinging. One is reminded of John Dryden's comment, in *Origin and Progress of Satire* (1692), distinguishing between invective (direct abuse) and verbal irony:

> How easy is it to call "rogue" and "villain," and that wittily. But how hard to make a man appear a fool, a blockhead, or a knave, without using any of those opprobrious terms.

Whether things have changed since 1971, when Brady's essay first appeared in *Ms.* Magazine, is a question that might be argued. One might also ask (though of course one doesn't expect a balanced view in satire) if things in 1971 really were the way Brady saw them. Did marriage really offer nothing to a wife? No love, no companionship, no security? Were all husbands childish and selfish, and all wives selfless?

Peter Singer

Animal Liberation (p. 311)

This essay is an earlier version of text that became the opening chapter of Peter Singer's remarkably influential *Animal Liberation: A New Ethics for Our Treatment of Animals* (1975). In his book, Singer elaborates all his basic ideas, and especially "speciesism" (para. 13), to which he devotes a whole chapter.

Speciesism is the arbitrary favorable preference for members of our own species, and its logical consequence is an equally arbitrary but indifferent or hostile attitude toward lower species. Whether the analogy to racism, sexism, and other *-isms* is as instructive as Singer implies is another matter. In any case, he argues (para. 19) that the "case for animal liberation" does not depend on the analogy.

What, then, is animal liberation? Singer never says in so many words (see para. 3), but it amounts to, or at least can be stated as, a series of Dos and Don'ts: Don't kill animals to eat their flesh or to clothe your body, don't experiment on animals to save human lives or to reduce human misery, don't remove animals from their yourself.

Singer's opening paragraph is a model for the use of analogy to gain the high ground right from the start. Each of his readers will be able to identify with one or another of the groups he mentions that has been discriminated against in the past and so is immediately but unwittingly vulnerable to the "expansion of our moral horizons" about to unfold.

Singer worries (para. 12; our question 3) whether having intentions is necessarily, albeit mysteriously, connected with having the capacity to use language. We doubt that it is, and he does, too. Surely anyone who spends time with dogs and cats readily ascribes intentions to them ("He's trying to catch the stick when you throw it," "She's waiting to pounce on the mouse as soon as it moves"), and this use of intentional thinking is no more anthropomorphic than is ascribing intentions to other people. To insist that the latter is intelligible but the former isn't, because other people can speak a language whereas animals can't, pretty obviously begs the question. To insist that no creature can have an intention unless it can state what its intentions are is far too broad a thesis to defend; it would entail that many human creatures do not have intentions, or act intentionally, when we believe they do. And so even if animals can't use language, because they lack the capacity, they may yet have minds enough to warrant a concern about how we intentionally treat them.

On what grounds does Singer base drawing the line where he does to demark the creatures that deserve our concern from those that don't? Why not draw the line elsewhere, particularly at the point that divides the living from the nonliving (not dead but inorganic or inert)? It wouldn't be at all satisfactory for Singer to answer: "Because I talk about creatures that can feel, and I don't about those that can't," although this reading seems to be true. But this can't be his answer because he does not want his argument to turn on who cares about what; he knows that most of us simply do not and will not easily come to care about animal welfare. A better line for him to take would be to refer to the *interests* of creatures and to the *equality* of their interests (para. 6), on the ground that only creatures with a capacity to suffer have interests, the first and foremost of which is to diminish their own suffering, pain, and discomfort. But on closer inspection, is it not still true that *all living* things have interests? Surely, a dogwood tree in the front yard has an interest in air, water, sunlight, and space to grow, even if it feels no pain when it is denied these things or when its leaves are plucked or — heaven forfend! — its branches slashed. To reason in this manner is to tie the concept of having an interest in something to the concept of something being good for a thing (water is surely good for a plant). But this is not what Singer does; rather, he ties a creature's interests to what it can feel (see how he handles the case of the year-old infant in para. 15).

When one goes in the other direction, as some have (for example, Christopher Stone, in his *Should Trees Have Standing?* [1988]), a whole environmental ethic begins to unfold, but with alarming consequences, for even all but the most scrupulous vegetarianism will neglect and even ruthlessly violate the interests of other living entities.

If we enlarge our moral community to include plants as well as animals — because all living entities have interests and because one interest is as good as another "from the point of view of the universe" (the criterion proposed by the utilitarian Henry Sidgwick, which Singer invokes in his *Animal Liberation*, 5) — what will our moral principles permit us to eat? Not much, perhaps only unfruitful food, such as some of the surfeit of seeds and nuts produced by plants, and dead flesh, perhaps including even human flesh (our question 10). Killing to eat may be entirely ruled out, but eating what is dead isn't unless one appeals to some other moral principles besides the utilitarian notions Singer relies on.

Garrett Hardin

Lifeboat Ethics: The Case against Helping the Poor (p. 326)

Garrett Hardin's essay is probably the most widely read and controversial of any that have attempted to alert the reading public to environmental dangers — indeed, catastrophes — that lie ahead if we (the affluent nations) continue on our current path of sticking on a Band-Aid here and there in response to famine, AIDS, and the other major killers in the third world. Hardin's great predecessor — the Reverend Thomas Malthus (1766–1834) — goes unmentioned in his essay. Two centuries ago, Malthus warned that population was increasing at an exponential rate, that food supply could increase only at a linear rate, that millions would eventually starve as the number of hungry mouths outstripped the capacity to feed them, and that the cycle would repeat itself endlessly.

At the heart of his argument is what he calls "the tragedy of the commons" (para. 15), a phrase he coined and a concept now invariably employed in the ongoing discussion of these issues. The idea is worth a closer look. A common is essentially anything owned and used by the community at large. Some commons are modest in scale, such as the grassy meadow in the center of a typical New England village used in earlier days for sheep and cattle grazing by any or all of the local herders. Others, like the air, seem virtually infinite in scope and therefore inexhaustible. What is tragic about a common is that without a social mechanism for protecting it from ruinous exploitation by who-ever gets there first, its exhaustion and destruction are inevitable. Uncontrolled population growth and unrestricted immigration merely speed up the process. In Hardin's own words, "If everyone would restrain himself, all would be well; but it takes only one less than every-one to ruin a system of voluntary restraint. . . . [M]utual ruin is inevitable if there are no controls" (para. 16). Perhaps Hardin would prefer (see paras. 1–3) that, like a spaceship, earth should be ruled by those with the authority to do so, including making the hard decisions on which collective survival depends.

To return to his analogy, if a lifeboat is treated as a common, it is bound to swamp, and all will perish. If it is treated as the private prop-erty of those who got into it first, then at least some will survive. To be sure, the survivors may not get in first but rather may get and keep a seat despite the pressure of others who take those seats for themselves. And while "First come, first served" may be a good principle for run-ning an Oklahoma land rush a century ago or for queuing at a ticket booth for tonight's movie, few will abide by it where their own lives are at stake: Voluntary adherence to the principle "First come" will be defeated in practice by those who choose to act on the principle "To the victor belongs the spoils."

Central to the debate over Hardin's tough-minded advice is the adequacy of his lifeboat analogy — that human life on planet earth is essentially like living on a lifeboat but that the constraints evident in the lifeboat are hidden and obscured in various ways in life on earth. We are disturbed by Hardin's ugly metaphor of the human race as a "cancerous growth" (para. 30, our question 6), but we cannot see how he is wrong in believing that unchecked growth in human population will eventually make human life and society as we know them today all but impossible. What is insidious, of course, is that the "cancer" is slow growing and piecemeal adjustments year after year mask its relentless progress. Is it unreasonable to hope that social factors Hardin neglects will cause human population growth to decline and that international legal controls will slowly but steadily make their presence felt, thereby keeping Lifeboat Earth afloat? We do not expect to be around to see for ourselves.

James Rachels

Active and Passive Euthanasia (p. 337)

Patients have the right to refuse treatment or any form of medical intervention; but they do not have the right to receive whatever treatment or intervention they demand. Consequently, as things currently stand, they do not have the right to ask (much less demand) that a doctor put them out of their misery. The right to refuse undoubtedly underlies the AMA's position that tolerates "cessation of . . . extraordinary means to prolong the life of the body," or "passive" euthanasia, but rejects "mercy killing" (and hence "active" euthanasia) because that involves acting with the "intention" to "terminate" the patient's life. This bears on our first question.

The essence of James Rachels's argument that active euthanasia is sometimes preferable to passive euthanasia (question 2) is essentially utilitarian. That is, he assumes the criterion of right conduct is reduction of human suffering; accordingly, letting someone die by slow starvation and dehydration (the result of withholding nourishment) may take longer, or otherwise be more painful, than directly injecting some lethal but painless drug.

Now one can argue against such a view in any of three ways. First, one can reject the utilitarian criterion or at least limit its application in this context. Second, one can challenge the factual premise, according to which it is more painful to be allowed to die than to be put to death. Third, one can concede both premises but insist that a utilitarian must take other things into account besides the pain and suffering of the dying person — such as whether the practice of directly killing the dying would result in "slippery slope" objections that might outweigh the good done through pain reduction in direct killing of the dying.

As we note in question 6, Rachels's main purpose is to destroy our commonsense confidence that "the bare difference between killing and letting die" makes "a moral difference." Rachels argues that "killing is not in itself any worse than letting die" (para. 16). His principal argument is based on a pair of hypothetical cases he carefully constructs in paragraphs 10 and 11, and his own discussion of these cases in paragraph 12. If your students are like ours, they will quickly get to the heart of the matter by discussing this pair of cases.

One might wonder, however, whether Rachels has proved his point. Has he shown that there is no *moral difference whatever* between killing and letting die — or only that *in certain cases*, like the hypothetical cases he invents, there is no moral difference? And isn't there an enormous range of cases of letting die, where the moral judgment to be placed on the person who lets another die varies with a range of obvious factors (risk to the bystander, cost and likely effectiveness of the intervention, fault of the dying person for his or her current plight)? But if this is true, then there are moral differences among cases of letting die; so perhaps one ought to be cautious in concluding that there are no moral differences whatever between a case of killing and a case of letting die.

As for the "mistake" (para. 14) that Rachels thinks the AMA makes in its position statement, which he quoted in his first paragraph, we are again not sure there is any such mistake. If a doctor at a patient's request withdraws further life support, Rachels says that such action is "the intentional termination of the life of one human being by another." Is it? Can't the doctor who accedes to the patient's request argue as follows: "To act as my patient requests, I withhold all further medical intervention with this patient. I believe the patient has made this request in the expectation that his death will result. I believe he is right." But does the action in question, based on the hypothesized beliefs, amount to *acting with the intention to terminate the patient's life*? It is not obvious that it does. For suppose that after the doctor ended medical intervention, the patient miraculously lived on painlessly. Would the doctor necessarily construe that happy event as an outcome contrary to his intentions? Not unless his intentions had been to murder the patient. But in the normal case of letting a patient die, the doctor had no such intentions, and so the happy miracle does not thwart his intentions at all.